CAP MOSSMAN: Last of the Great Cowmen

CAP MOSSMAN
Last of the Great Cowmen

BY

FRAZIER HUNT

WITH SIXTEEN ILLUSTRATIONS BY

ROSS SANTEE

HASTINGS HOUSE

Publishers   New York

To

RUTH SHRADER MOSSMAN

*Whose gracious hospitality
and kindness had so much to do
with making the task of gathering
this material a happy one*

CAP MOSSMAN: Last of the Great Cowmen

Cowboy and Ramrod

THE TERRITORY of New Mexico was a rough and violent land when the Mossman family arrived in 1882.

It didn't take much pressure for a strong-willed boy to go bad and join up with the wild bunch. Many people felt certain that would be the end of the oldest boy, Burt.

But somehow he managed to squeeze through the various fights and quarrels he had without having to kill a man. His initiation into the Southwest, however, was a pretty tough one.

He had just turned twenty when he crossed from the east side of the Rio Grande to the mountainous country of the great cattle spreads. For three years he had been working on small ranches, and he had thoroughly learned his trade. But this would be his first real roundup.

He would never forget that first sight he had of the three chuck wagons strung along Palomas creek. They'd pulled in only a few hours before and the wagons had parked two or three hundred feet from one another.

It was late afternoon when Burt rode up. The three cook fires were going and the men were sitting around on their heels, or sprawled out on the ground with their backs against their bedrolls. A mile or two away grazed the remudas, each with eighty or ninety horses.

He recognized Henry Street, the round-up captain, leaning against one of the high rear wheels of the first chuck wagon. Dropping off his string of horses, he rode straight up to him.

Warren Carpenter, the ranch manager of the Bar A Bar, had warned him about Street being a gun-fighter with a hot temper. Maybe that was what nettled the boy even before he'd stepped down from his horse. He knew he wasn't going to like this tall, powerfully built Texan.

"I'm the rep from the Bar A Bar," Burt slowly pronounced.

Street let his insolent gray eyes take in the slight figure of the boy. He wouldn't weigh more than a hundred and thirty-five pounds and he'd have to stretch himself to stand five feet seven.

"You the son of that damnyankee major named Mossman from below Las Crucas?" Street gruffly asked.

"My father was one of the men who licked the hell out of you rebels, if that's what you mean." Burt's eyes were blazing. Street's right hand dropped to his hip. It had slipped his mind that his Colt was in his bedroll.

He'd like to pistol-whip this young squirt. He sure needed a good working over.

"So you're hankerin' for trouble, are you?" the older man demanded.

"No, but I ain't runnin' away from it."

Street jerked down the brim of his black felt hat. "It's too bad we got a rule against fightin' on roundups," he said. "I reckon I'll have to wait to take care of your case, Mossman."

"Suit yourself," Burt answered.

Street hesitated and then went on: "Turn your horses in the remuda over there. Then get something to eat."

Burt watched the Texan walk over toward the cook fire. He still wished he could tangle with the big fellow. He'd whipped bigger men. If you were tough and fast, and knew how to hit and let the haymakers slide off your shoulder, size didn't make much difference.

He'd promised Warren Carpenter he'd have no trouble with Street, and he realized it would have been wrong to crawl the bully. He'd just file that happy moment for later consideration. What he wanted now was experience, and he could afford to nurse along this two-bit grudge fight.

As a matter of fact, Burt had done mighty well learning how to control his hair-trigger temper. Charlie Wall, ramrod of the little Hat ranch on east of the river where he'd got his first job as a cowboy, used to talk with him a lot about that. Charlie warned him plenty that someday he'd kill a man and even if a jury turned him loose he'd have the mark on him all his life. Once a fellow was branded as a killer there were plenty of men in the wild bunch waiting to try him out.

His father, too, was always lecturing him about his temper and his constant fighting. The senior Mossman was quite a man himself: he'd enlisted in the Fighting 36th Illinois Volunteers as a twenty-one-year-old private when it was recruited, and he was mustered out as a major, with four battle wounds. Shortly after he left the army he married a farm girl named Anna West, and Burt was born April 30th, 1867. When he was six the family moved from the farm near Aurora, Illinois, to Lake City, Minnesota.

Three years later Burt and his father drove two prairie schooners two hundred miles west to two claims his father had near Marshall. That was just thirty miles from the Dakota border, and it was the same summer that General Custer and part of his Seventh Cavalry were rubbed out by the Sioux and Cheyennes at the Little Big Horn.

Burt's folks on both sides were fine, sturdy Scotch-Irish

pioneer stock. His Grandfather West had driven oxen out to the Illinois country in 1841. Burt's father had come west from Marietta, Ohio, when he was a young fellow. They never could figure out where this oldest boy, Burt, got his wild, restless streak, but he sure had it.

His mother used to worry about him a lot. It wasn't that she thought he was really mean; he was only hot-tempered and full of the Old Harry.

But he was honest and trustworthy, and when he made up his mind to do something, he never gave up. When he was sixteen he swam the Rio Grande at the top of a spring flood to get the payroll for the Mexicans working on his father's big irrigation ditch. Burt had learned to talk Spanish fluently and he was a sort of straw boss and helped pay off Saturday nights.

The $228 in silver that Burt strapped around his waist in a money belt weighed fourteen pounds. When he started to swim back to the left bank the river had risen, and the heavy silt got in around the money belt.

He was gulping water and the waves were rolling over his head before he was half-way across. He reached down to jerk off the belt.

Then he changed his mind. The Mossmans couldn't afford to lose that money. He'd stay with it, no matter what happened.

Suddenly he felt himself being swept downstream, and he drew in a big chunk of air, and let the current carry him along. His head cleared, and he knew he'd make it somehow or other. Before long he could hear his father shouting to him, and then his feet struck bottom on the opposite bank, and the Major was wading out to him.

The Major was mighty proud of his son and he tried his best to make him a partner in his plans for a great irrigation ditch that would carry the muddy waters of the big river the nine miles to the Texas line. But handling a shovel was far too tame for Burt, and when he was still sixteen he started working with a surveying crew in the dangerous, Apache-infested Sacramento mountains, on east of the waterless Tularosa Basin.

One boiling hot June day the boss suddenly realized that he had to get his official Washington reports off on the next mail from the stage stop on the east slope of the Organs, 55 miles across the Tularosa Basin. There wasn't a horse or mule in the outfit that could make the journey in time, so Burt volunteered to try it on foot.

He started at three o'clock that morning and by nine o'clock that night he'd walked the 55 miles over the boiling sands, with the only available water at a dripping spring in the pass through the dwarf Jarilla Mountains, half-way across. He mailed his documents at eight that following morning, and then started the long, hard grind back. He pulled in around two in the morning.

He'd done 110 miles on foot in the hot desert in a total time-spread of 47 hours. He might have a wild temper and like to fight, but he sure had what it took when it came to finishing up anything he started.

All that year he was out with the surveyors he was dreaming of being a cowboy. When the outfit was disbanded he chiseled himself a job on the little Hat ranch, at the Five Springs near the stage stop where he'd delivered the mail on his big walk.

Burt lasted a year under Charlie Wall, the tall, pleasant foreman, and before he let his temper betray him into a battle with an older hand that might easily have ended with one of them being killed, Burt had become a pretty fair cowboy. He blew the next three jobs, and then rode across the river and headed northwest for the big outfits, where he could really learn the cowboy trade.

Warren Carpenter, whose Bar A Bar ran back west of the river and north from the cow camp at Hot Springs, gave the boy a trying-out as a bog rider. Rescuing the big stuff from the treacherous, gray quicksand was the meanest and nastiest job on a ranch, but Burt didn't kick. He'd never quit trying to save a critter, and the ranch manager liked his honesty and persever- ance. At the end of a few weeks Carpenter sent him to repre- sent the Bar A Bar on the big roundup under Street.

The sun was popping over the horizon when the round-up captain led the men off to the southwest. All told, there were

some thirty-five riders, and they would gather and brand only calves and maverick yearlings.

The riders dropped out of the cavalcade one at a time, roughly a half-mile apart, forming a great net that faced the north. Each man rode back and forth across the area assigned to him, making certain that no smart old cow had her calf hidden in a clump of mesquite or in some concealed draw.

If a cow had no calf at her side the rider would slip up close

enough to get a good look at her bag. If she was being sucked he knew that she had cached her calf somewhere in the rear, and it was up to him to find it and bring on the two of them.

Long before the round-up grounds were in sight each man's batch had grown to considerable proportions. Oddly enough the bigger the catch the easier it was for the rider to handle it.

When Burt topped a rise with his batch of thirty or forty head, a thrilling panorama spread out before him. From all sides cows and calves were trailing into the creek valley below. There was a continuous bellowing, and now and again the trumpet call of some old bull who insisted on going along. Dust rose in moving ribbons as the long lanes of cattle flowed into the holding grounds, as if drawn together by some mysterious, all-powerful magnet.

Burt was tired and thirsty and hungry, but he was filled with a sense of deep satisfaction. He was no longer working for some obscure little outfit, operating on the fringes of the vast industry. He belonged.

The red sun was hanging low when the last of the calves was dragged up to the branding fire. Half-way through the long ordeal, Burt and his partner in the calf-wrestling had been relieved and sent out to help hold the cows and calves that belonged to the reps. Some days later, when these numbered several hundred head, they would be driven to their various home ranges.

But on this first night the hundred or so head of the neighboring outfits would be held in a loose herd. One man on night guard was enough, and the reps arranged among themselves which two-hour shift each would take. Burt drew the ten to midnight. He wouldn't have to stand guard the following night.

He and Cole Railston spread out their blankets as soon as supper was over, and it didn't seem to Burt that he'd been asleep more than twenty minutes before someone was shaking him. He had chosen a bright little bay for his night horse, and he had him tied to a mesquite a dozen feet away. He tightened the cinch and stepped up.

Overhead the big, low-hanging southern stars were cracking and blinking. Off to the right the herd was as quiet as sleeping soldiers at midnight. Some of the cows were lying down, with their calves curled up nearby.

The bay pony started circling, just as if he'd been doing it all his life. Warren Carpenter had told him to be sure to use Sleepy Red for his night horse. Burt tied his split reins together and hung the loop over his saddle horn.

First thing he knew he woke up with a start. Old Sleepy Red was still circling. Burt guessed it was that coyote way off up the creek that had awakened him.

He recalled the little row he'd had with Street. He could afford to take it easy and learn all that he could now.

Mister Street would keep.

-- 2 --

Burt did not see his boss, Warren Carpenter, again until mid-July, when he brought in the last batch of Bar A Bar stuff to the home range along the Canada Alamosa.

For six weeks Warren had been out with his own wagon working the country to the north and west, in conjunction with Bill Hardin's Anchor X wagon. Warren was at the corrals when Burt rode in, and the boss told him to come on up to the house and meet his brother Andy, who owned a chunk of the Bar A Bar and was going to take over its management. He explained that he'd had a fancy offer to run the Bar N Cross's and he'd taken it. Andy had just come down from Pueblo, Colorado.

"I'd like to go along with you," Burt blurted out.

Warren quietly explained that it wouldn't be right to leave Andy with nothing but this bunch of meat-heads around the ranch. Warren was always referring to people he didn't like as meat-heads: he said a meat-head was a fellow whose head was all meat and no bone, with the neck just growing up and hairing over.

Andy was three or four years older than Warren, but Burt saw right away that he wasn't half the man his younger brother was. Still, he was pleasant and he said to Burt he wanted him to be his head rider. He was going to raise his wages to forty-five dollars a month.

When Warren left, Andy seemed to enjoy talking over the cattle business with Burt. He told him all about the great drives up the Texas Trails in the late Sixties and Seventies, and how foreign investors poured in millions of dollars in northern ranches, and how the big Cattle Boom began to blow up in '84, just about the time the Bar A Bar was started. From then on cattle prices began to slide downhill. Northern ranges were heavily overstocked and the whole industry was loaded with cheap cattle.

Andy went on to explain how dry the previous summer of '86 had been, especially in the north, and how millions of stockers had gone into the winter in poor shape. Fall storms were followed by warm weather, and then early in January, of this year of '87, the worst blizzard in the history of the northern cow country had swept down. A chinook melted off a few inches of top snow, but hard weather immediately closed in and thousands of square miles of cured grass in the upper High Plains lay under a thick crust of ice until the spring that had just passed unlocked it.

Northern ranges lost up to 90 percent of their stock, and some of the biggest outfits didn't even bother to gather the pitiful few that remained. Then to this unprecedented loss of life came the complete collapse in prices. The great cattle industry was broke, and even here in the southern breeding grounds things looked bad.

"Just stay with cows long enough and they'll break any man," Andy continued. "Bad weather and low prices—those are the enemies that never let up on a cattleman. Either one is tough enough, but when they join together you're finished."

Burt never forgot that bit of wisdom.

-- 3 --

It was mid-August when a terrific electric storm ushered in a heavy rain. That same night Cole Railston, who was just forty days older than Burt, galloped up to the ranch with the news that Andy's brother, Warren Carpenter, had been killed by lightning. Burt rode alongside of Andy that night, and it was just coming dawn when they reached the Bar N Cross headquarters.

The boys had been working all night on the coffin. As soon as they had breakfast a bunch of them started for Engle Station on the Santa Fé, riding alongside the wagon that carried Warren's homemade casket. Just before the train arrived Andy Carpenter took Burt to one side.

"I'm making you foreman," he said quietly. "You're in full charge until I get back."

Burt could only gulp out his thanks when he shook hands and said good-bye to his boss.

It was hard to believe—foreman of an outfit of 8,000 head and barely turned twenty-one!

He wished his father and mother knew about it right this

14

minute. His mother would cry a little, and his father would scratch his beard and call him a good soldier.

On the way back to the ranch he wanted to tell Cole Railston and the boys who'd ridden over to the Santa Fé with the wagon, but he just couldn't do it. Somehow he couldn't help but feel that the death of his friend Warren, who'd given him his chance on the Bar A Bar, had something to do with his getting the job.

For his sake he'd try as hard as he could to make good. In his wildest dreams he'd never thought he'd have such good luck as to ramrod an outfit of 8,000 by the time he turned twenty-one.

He sure had his work cut out for him!

Burt branded 2,500 calves that summer, doing the big end of the calf roping himself. The Lankford Brothers, who owned most of the spread, wrote the young foreman how pleased they were. Andy Carpenter was likewise sincere in his congratulations. He had a fifth interest in the outfit and he was figuring on completely turning the management over to Burt as soon as expedient.

Most of that next winter Andy spent with his family in Colorado, and Burt was in actual charge of the ranch. He was settling down in fine shape, and the last thing he was looking for was trouble.

Most of the people in the neighborhood were Spanish-speaking and he got along fine with them, partly because he talked the language fluently.

Things were dry and Burt spent a good deal of time riding alone over the ranges and doing what he could for the cattle. The village of Monticello was two miles up the Canada Alamosa from the ranch, and on this particular night when he rode through the dirt plaza on his way home he was tired and worried about the lack of grass and water. He drank no hard liquor at all but he figured a nice cold bottle of Mexican beer right now would taste mighty good.

Two or three ponies were at the tie rack in front of the village *cantina* when he pulled up and dismounted. He could hear angry voices as he pushed through the swinging door. In the dim light at the rear of the big room he could see Juan Reyes, a harmless little sheepherder he happened to know, struggling with a local tough and gambler who was almost twice his size. Juan was down and the bully was kicking him when Burt stepped up and shoved back the big Mexican.

"Whatcha tryin' to do, kill him?" Burt demanded.

"Ugh!" the Mexican grunted. "You want some too, ugh? You Gringo *cabrón!*"

Burt let the punch slide off his shoulder and hit him with his right hand. It staggered the big man, and Burt saw him reach for his knife. The American lashed out at him.

Burt's right uppercut caught him on the point of the jaw and when he hit the floor Burt was on him. His fingers tightened around the bull neck of the tough. When the spectators got Burt to loosen up, the gambler's tongue was sticking out of his mouth.

Burt did not bother with his bottle of beer. One of his old Spanish-speaking friends begged him to leave before there was more trouble.

"Thees *hombre* he ees bad man," the native told Burt. "You must be veery careful or he weel keel you, *amigo.*"

But Burt wasn't worried. It had been his first fight in several months and he'd enjoyed it. If the big Mex wanted any more he'd be glad to accommodate him at any time he wished.

A few nights later Burt returned to the ranch after a long and disheartening ride over to the west of his range. Cows and calves were thin and it looked bad. He was mounted on a white pony, and for some reason he did not follow his usual custom of riding along the pasture fence, next the row of peach trees, to the gate a hundred yards away. Ordinarily he took off his saddle and bridle there, swung them over the top rail of the gate and let the pony into the alfalfa.

But this night he was tired and worried, and he unsaddled at the corral directly in front of the house and turned Whitey loose. He knew that early the next morning when the boy jingled in the horses he would find the pony at the pasture gate and let him on in to graze.

After supper he sat down at his desk by the open window of the room he shared with John Lacy. John was sleeping in a homemade bed in the far corner of the room, while Burt was busy writing to the owners in Pueblo about the bad state of affairs. A lighted lamp was on the table in front of Burt.

Some unaccountable subconscious sense suddenly caused Burt to lift his head. That tenth of a second a heavy bullet crashed into the lamp-chimney, throwing broken glass in his face. It would have gone through his forehead had he not raised his head. The slug cut through the bedstead, missing Lacy by a matter of inches.

Burt sprang to his feet, pulled out his six-shooter from its holster hanging on the back of a chair near his cot, and rushed out through the open hall into the dark night. He searched around the corrals and the stables but he could locate no trace of his assailant.

The following morning he and Lacy found footprints of a man near the steel wheel of a horse-drawn mower that was parked a few feet from the open window. Apparently the attacker had at first hidden himself behind the row of peach trees, with the idea of killing Burt when he rode along the pasture to turn his pony loose in the alfalfa field.

But Burt had unsaddled his pony at the corrals, and the

would-be murderer, thwarted in his original plan, waited until
Burt had finished his supper and taken his seat in the bedroom
alongside the lighted lamp. The thing that had saved his life
was the sudden raising of his head.

Burt was morally certain that the Mexican bully and gambler
in Monticello had done the job, but there was no way he could
prove it. He promised himself that the first chance he had he'd
pick a quarrel with him and then kill the coward out of hand.
It was the only way he could be sure of not being ambushed a
second time.

Word of the attempted murder seeped up and down the
Green Canyon and a few days after the incident Bill Hardin,
wagon boss of the Anchor X on up north, decided he'd jog
down and get the story straight from Burt. Hardin was a first
cousin of John Wesley Hardin, the most famous gun-fighter
Texas ever produced. Bill was no slouch himself as a scrapper.
When he rode away from his ranch he told the manager, an
Easterner whom most of the hands cordially disliked, that he'd
be gone for the day. The Anchor X, incidentally, was partly
owned by the famous Chicago lawyer and agnostic, Col. Robert
Ingersoll.

About half-way on down the Alamosa from the Anchor X lay
the irrigated vineyard of Alphonso Bourgett, a Frenchman married to a Mexican. When Bill pulled up his horse and bid them
a *buenos días,* Alphonso asked him to come in and have a glass
of wine.

It seemed a fair proposition to the slow-speaking, lanky Texan,
and he followed his host into the dirt cellar under the adobe
house. It was a long room, and along the sides were parked
some seventy or eighty barrels of wine. The two men were
enjoying their second glass when they were joined by the
gambler from Monticello who had tangled with Burt.

After a few friendly drinks of wine the host brought out a

bottle of brandy that he had distilled for his own use. It was cleaned up shortly, and a second bottle appeared. The wine was heady and the brandy was powerful, and before many hours had slipped by both the Mexican and the Texan were very much the worse for wear. Man-made restraints gave way and the ancient enmities between the two races flashed out in bold relief.

There were violent words passed and the Mexican reached for the knife that he carried in a scabbard looped to his belt. At the gesture Hardin drew his pistol and the slug from his Colt tore through the Mexican's head.

Befuddled and blazing with hate, Hardin stumbled upstairs, found his horse and turned northward toward the Anchor X. His unconscious instincts told him that if he didn't make tracks he'd be caught in the wild rage of a race war.

Hardin was galloping his horse when the animal stumbled and he was thrown. When he got to his feet his horse was hitting it for home.

Hardin's reflexes started him walking up the rough narrow road toward the ranch house and temporary safety. Two miles on north he came to the shack of John Cloudman. He found some cold biscuit and a piece of boiled beef, and as he was leaving he picked up John's rifle. He was sure the boys at the ranch would come for him as soon as his riderless horse reached the corrals.

He started on up the trail again, but his tight, high-heeled cowboy boots pinched his feet, and he was terribly tired. Off to the left, on up a steep slope, he caught sight of a gnarled old cedar tree. He managed to climb up and settle back against it so that he could watch the trail his friends would use when they came to get him. In a minute he was lost in a heavy alcoholic sleep.

Two hours later the mob trailed his steps to the cabin of

John Cloudman, and then followed them on up the road. A famous rifle shot named Juan Boca led the gang. Juan hated all Texans and he saw his chance to even up matters.

A mile or two on up the trail he spied the sleeping figure. His first shot tore off half his head. The rest of the men crowded around the dead Hardin and emptied their weapons into him.

The next morning when Burt and a half-dozen others rode up the trail the frightened wife of the old Frenchman sobbed out the story.

"Nevair have I see such a *pobrecito*," she stammered. "He is shot maybe forty time."

Hardin had saved Burt a lot of trouble, but it had gone mighty tough with the tall, pleasant Texan.

Maybe people were only partly responsible for what they did, Burt mused as he rode home in the gathering twilight.

-- 4 --

Every day now Burt would sniff the air and study the white, cloudless sky. Not a single winter or spring rain broke the frightening monotony. Water-holes and springs were low and living water was beginning to dry up.

The calf crop at the June gather and branding was a good third less than it had been the year before. But Burt felt sure rain would soon come. Miracles could happen in the New Mexico land, and he figured there'd be sufficient browse until the summer rains broke.

Andy showed up some time after June branding was over, with instructions that Burt ship out the big end of the yearlings and two-year-old steers early that fall. The young foreman pushed forward his late branding, and gathered 1,800 head of young stuff. Then he rode over to Engle to arrange for three stock trains. Two would go to a siding near Pueblo where the Lankfords had a big fattening pasture. Burt would personally take the third train to Dodge City.

Four days later he and the cowboys crossed the herd at the Engle Ford. They started loading the cars shortly after daybreak, and by four that afternoon they were finished. It was hard, sweaty work, twisting tails and shoving and shouting and poking cattle up the chutes and into cars. Being a lowly "cow-poke" was quite a comedown from the proud status of a lordly "cowboy."

Burt rode out with the last train, and it was a big moment for him when he swung up to the platform of the caboose—a full-fledged ranch foreman delivering a trainload of beef he had personally gathered and trailed and loaded. This was the real thing.

Two days after leaving Engle, the train pulled in at Dodge City. Burt got himself cleaned up and bought a checked suit of clothes, a ten-dollar hat and a pair of fancy boots, and then gaily went forth to do the town. He bucked two roulette wheels, played a little faro, sat in a steep poker game, and had a few dances. But the fact that he didn't drink the hard stuff was like a safety valve on his big evening.

The next morning he was, nevertheless, a little the worse for wear, and he was glad to pull out for Pueblo. Mr. Garrett Lankford, the senior of the brothers who owned the ranch, had invited him to pay his family a visit on his way home.

It was an eye-opener for the young wagon boss. He was never to forget how gracious his hostess was, nor how impressed he was when she led him over the great house, with its genuine oil paintings, its dark paneled library and long dining-room, with the silver and crystal gleaming and glistening like frozen sleet on the trees up north.

After supper when they were seated in the parlor, Mr. Lankford asked him a hundred and one questions about the Bar A Bar, the state of the grass and water, and the general condition of the cattle. Burt didn't try to minimize the desperate future they faced if the dry-up continued.

Mr. Lankford told him that he was making him permanent range manager and that his salary would be $100 a month. He was sorry he couldn't make it more, but Burt would have to realize what bad shape financially the ranch was in. He would have full responsibility from now on, and it was up to him to make good.

Burt could not help but feel proud of himself but he was considerably worried as he rode the Santa Fé south. If the drouth continued the jig was up. Cattle couldn't live without water and grass and browse. And if there was a disastrous dry-up it wouldn't be his fault, but he'd get the blame, just the same.

-- 5 --

Back at the ranch Burt tried his best not to let the sight or sound of the hungry starving cows and calves ruin his days and nights. Only the native ranchers, with their tiny farms scattered along the irrigation ditches, seemed able to endure the endless procession of days without rain. They would cross themselves and mumble sacred names when he would pull up his horse and talk to them.

The scanty round-up that early summer was finished well before the first of July. There was little mood for play, but that winter there had been friendly banter about which outfit would have the champion steer roper at the Fourth of July celebration to be held on up the river at San Marcial. Henry Street and Cole Railston and the boys to the south bragged that they were backing a boy named Jimmy Long against the field. They knew that Burt fancied a Mexican vaquero named Antanasio Vasques who worked for him during the round-ups.

Antanasio was squat and thick-chested, and he didn't look as if he could move fast enough to get out of his own shadow. But Burt knew differently. The Mexican was not only sure-fire with his rope but he was incredibly fast getting off his horse and up to his steer, once he had busted him. His powerful arms moved like an automatic vise when he pulled the noose of his piggin' string around the two back feet of a critter and then forced them forward so he could get the loop around a fore front and make his half-hitch.

Antanasio talked a little too much and got drunk at every possible opportunity, but Burt knew he had a champion in this man, trained on one of the great ranches of Old Mexico. Burt's main problem would be to keep him in shape until after the roping contest was over.

The previous summer Burt had traded for a little sorrel pony named Vic that was the fastest and most intelligent roping horse he had ever ridden. The split-second he would make his horn-catch, and then racing alongside flip the rope over the critter's back, the pony would whirl to the left and keep his feet when the animal hit the end of the maguey and turned a somersault. Both Burt and his vaquero practiced roping off Vic.

Henry Street claimed that the Mexican was breaking too many horns when he would bust critters that June round-up, and he and Burt almost got into a fight over it. But Cole Railston interfered and things calmed down. Unquestionably the big Mexican was rough on steers and hard on horses, and Burt rather hated to have him ride his little sorrel.

There was general holiday in all the countryside when the first week of July swung around. It was so dry and sweltering that a man had to prime himself to spit, as Cole Railston observed. Burt and most of his crew, with their Mexican champion in tow, jogged over to San Marcial the afternoon before the big celebration. They led Vic and hit a slow gait.

That night of July third was a pretty wild one. Burt bucked a poker game, and there was a full evening of drinking and miscellaneous quarreling and fighting. Burt tried to keep an eye on his squat Mexican, but he lost sight of him long before midnight. When he last saw him he was bucking a monte game in a Mexican *cantina* and was fairly sober. Burt reminded his protégé that he had put up the ten dollars for his entrance fee in the steer roping, and that he and the Bar A Bar boys were betting their shirts on him.

Burt got to bed an hour or two after midnight and early the following morning he was down in the dining-room of the hotel having his breakfast. Suddenly the morning calm was shattered by a pistol shot. Burt counted five in a row. It was a tell-tale number: a man carried exactly five live cartridges in his six-shooter, the hammer always resting on an empty shell.

It flashed through his mind that all the shooting had been done by one gun. Maybe it was only some drunk emptying his Colt into the tinted sky of the early morning.

Burt was finishing his coffee when Cole Railston pushed his way into the dining-room. He was grinning when he came up to Burt.

"Reckon you better git yo'sef another Mexican," he drawled. "That pet roper of yourn sure's had awful bad luck."

Burt hurried across the plaza to the alley behind the row of adobe buildings. A little crowd was looking down at a figure lying in the dust.

It was Burt's prize Mexican, right enough. He'd had a drunken argument with another Mexican and he'd got four slugs through the guts and one through the head before he gave up trying to get his knife working.

Burt went to the committee and asked them to let him rope in the Mexican's place. Then he announced that the bets he'd made on the Mexican would ride.

Jimmy Long's backers were smugly sitting back and covering all bets on Jimmy against the field. It simmered down to six of one and a half-dozen of the other: six on Jimmy and a half-dozen on Burt. The rest of the contestants were ordinary ropers and no one paid any attention to them.

Jimmy drew the first steer and plenty of hard luck. He missed his throw and he had to build himself a second loop. This time he made a perfect catch, busted his steer hard and was off his horse and had him tied down in perfect shape. The crowd groaned when the time was announced: one minute and forty-seven seconds.

Several Mexican ropers followed but the best time any of them made was around a minute.

Burt heard his own name called and he pulled up the cinch on his saddle and spoke to Vic. He could see the men driving his mossy horn to the starting lane.

The steer had a forty-foot start, but little Vic ate up the distance as if he'd been shot out of a cannon. Everything broke perfectly for Burt. He busted his steer so hard he was able to make his tie-down as fast as his hands could move.

The crowd went wild when the announcer called the time at twenty-four seconds. There was no such thing then as regular contest rules and regulations, but it was about as near a new world's record as a man could get.

That evening he refused a score of drinks. His pockets were full of cigars and his belly full of pop, and he had a right to feel well satisfied with himself.

It was getting toward midnight when Burt and Cole Railston and Gene Rhodes walked up to the hotel bar near where Henry Street was standing. The surly range manager had on a good-sized load, and when Burt ordered a soft drink, Street looked him up and down and remarked to the bartender that he ought to keep milk on tap for punks who hadn't been weaned.

Burt walked up close to the insulting Texan. The boy was thirty pounds lighter, and a good ten years younger. His tormentor had the thumbs of both hands tucked in his cartridge belt, and the butt of his heavy Colt wasn't three inches from the fingers of his right hand.

"Listen, Street," Burt said, his voice rising slowly. "You got a gun on and I'm not packing one. But anytime you're within ten feet of me I dare you to draw on me."

The blood was draining from Burt's face and his voice was hard and threatening, as he continued: "Why, I'd tear your heart out before you could move! I'd break your neck, you big fake!"

It was bitter medicine for the ranch manager to take. But there was something about this ball of fire standing in front of him that made him as dangerous as a den of rattlesnakes.

This boy wasn't afraid of him, gun or no gun. And Street knew he had his number.

Slowly Burt turned on his heels and walked to a poker table at the back end of the room. He was sure he'd never have any more trouble with Henry Street.

-- 6 --

All that summer a pitiless sun beat down, and there was little water and no feed. Even the browse was worthless.

Day after day Burt forced himself to ride over the scorched ranges. It made a lump come up in his throat when he'd see a gaunt old cow, so thin and weak she could hardly drag herself along, yet trailed by a calf still strong enough to throw up its head and high-tail it out of there when he'd ride close up. These Texas and Chihuahua cows sure were wonderful mothers.

In October a letter arrived instructing him to gather and ship out every yearling and two-year-old, steers and heifers alike, that was strong enough to travel as far as the railroad at Engle.

He was getting together his crew when Gene Rhodes rode in one evening just at supper time. Gene was the son of old Major Rhodes who for many years had been Indian agent for the Mescalero Apache Reservation. The Major was running a small cattle outfit in the San Andres Mountains, and Gene—who used the rather fancy handle of Eugene Manlove Rhodes—was trying to sell stories and poems to papers and magazines.

Gene explained that he and an old prospector had stumbled on a fine hidden spring at the foot of a tree stump in a lonely

spot on the west slope of the San Andres range. It was miles from any other water and consequently there was plenty of grass and pea vine all around it. He'd rent Burt his rights on the spring and the surrounding range for $100 a month. Gene had told no one of the find, and he assured Burt that there was enough water and feed there to take care of a thousand head of stock.

It sounded like a fairy tale to Burt but he agreed to leave the next day and look it over. If Burt would take the spring Gene said he'd enroll at the new college over in Silver City that fall. He was going to be a writer in spite of hell or high water.

They spent that first night at the cabin of the man who ran Engle Ferry, and dawn was just breaking when they pushed off across the thirty-mile dry *Jornada del Muerto* to the foothills of the San Andres. Burt had a five-gallon kerosene tin strapped on the back of his saddle.

It was late afternoon when they pulled it. They reopened the spring and the boys watered themselves and their famished mounts. The next morning Burt dug down with a shovel and when the water seeped up he filled and refilled his five-gallon tin, timing each operation, until he got a fair idea of the amount of the flow. He agreed he'd make the try, and pay Gene a hundred a month as long as his cattle used the spring.

He started back across the *Jornada* late that afternoon, and it was dark as the inside of a cow by the time he reached Engle Station. He put up his horse and caught the morning train going north. At Socorro he got a carpenter and his helper to build him eighty feet of red cypress troughs, a foot deep by two feet wide, and hustled them to the south-bound freight.

He had some difficulty hiring a team and wagon at Engle, but by dark that night he drew up at the secret spring. There was an abandoned stone shack a mile on up the mountain-slope from the spring, and he'd posted Gene there to hold this claim by the might of his rifle. Water was life, and this was squarely a matter of life or death. He had a chance to save a thousand of his starving steers, and he'd fight for that chance.

The following morning he set the eighty feet of troughs in a single straight line below the spring. Then he put a gooseneck piece of two-inch lead pipe, that he'd bought in Socorro, deep into the spring. Using his kerosene tin filled with water, he managed to start a syphon working. In a matter of minutes he had his long line of tanks filled and running over.

Whittling out a round piece of cedar the size of the pipe, he cut a notch in it about as big as a lead-pencil. Then he drove the plug into the end of the pipe syphon that rested in the first trough. A little experimenting gave him the exact flow that would keep the troughs full when the cattle were around. Then he took out the syphon, hid it, and started for the river and home.

He knew he'd be flatly disobeying orders not to ship out the cattle that were already being gathered. But a lot of them couldn't even stand the drive to the railroad, and the owners would not net $5 a head from the rest, after the freight charges were paid.

It was worth being fired to make this big gamble. He knew there'd be plenty of water at the secret spring, and the range for six or eight miles around hadn't been grazed for years. Even here in the heart of this terrible dry-up there'd be feed enough to save the dying stock and put tallow on their sunken frames.

With any sort of luck there ought to be a clear extra profit of not less than $10,000 within six months. Back at the ranch the cattle were dying like flies. He just couldn't pass up this chance to make a lick for the outfit.

When he reached home he found that his brother Dana and the boys had already gathered several hundred head of the sorriest-looking bunch of jack-rabbits any man ever saw. He hired three or four extra men to hurry up the job. Within a week he had better than a thousand head ready.

He had to move them slowly, and he put Dana on the drags so as to be sure the weak, stumbling critters would not drop off and be left behind. He bedded down the herd after a ten-mile drive. The next day he found the Rio Grande practically dry, and he crossed on the hard gravel of Engle Ford. That night he threw the herd into circle on the far side of the pass.

By bribes, threats and pleadings he managed to water the herd at the railroad yards at Engle station, and toward the late after-noon he started the thirty-mile dry drive across the *Jornada.*

He'd heard rumors that there was supposed to be some kind of an eclipse of the moon, but he was hardly prepared for the ter-rifying spectacle that presented itself a little before midnight, as he plodded across the wide, treacherous desert. He was riding at point and as the black curtain slowly began to close over the face of the full moon, it was as if a pall of doom was being drawn over it. Even the low stars seemed to be blinking in wonder and amazement.

Finally the great white ball was totally blacked out, and the universe stood motionless and in doubt. Then the bright edge of the moon began peering out and soon the silent land was once again bathed in its warm magic.

Burt was awed, but he had no time to indulge his mood. His problem was close at hand. His worry was whether this herd of hungry, thirsty, weakened cattle could last until he could get them to the troughs at the secret spring, on the other side of the waterless *Jornada.*

Burt was still watching the cattle enjoy the grass and pea vine and the wonderful water, when Gene started off to the new school at Silver City "to git educated." Dana Mossman was to stay on and look after the herd, but he arranged to ride along to Engle station and bring back Gene's horse. Burt decided he'd go with them as far as the railroad, on his way to the ranch.

Burt never saw Gene again, but he proudly followed his distinguished writing career. When Gene died in California in 1934, his wife brought back his body and he was buried under a cairn of rocks high up in the San Andres Mountains, overlooking the western world he loved so much.

"Paso por aquí" she had graved on the headstone. It was the title of one of his most beloved stories. He had done just that— "HE PASSED HERE."

Time flowed over Eugene Manlove Rhodes, just as time and the great Elephant Butte Dam eventually flowed over the useful Engle Ford, and the Engle Ferry. All three joined the never-never-land of memory.

-- 7 --

Burt tried his best not to let the sight or sound of the few hundred head of starving cows at the home ranch ruin his days and nights. The drouth had been on for three years now, and when the young range manager would look up at the hot empty sky he wondered what sort of God there was Who would let innocent dumb beasts endure such tortures of hunger and thirst as these animals were suffering. Only the yearlings and two-year-olds he had driven to Rhodes Spring managed to keep going.

Burt was beginning to believe that it never would rain again. Then early on the afternoon of July 2nd dark clouds began to race across the horizons, and there were strange mutterings and portents. Lightning flashed and thunder rolled as if the sky were suffering heroic birth pains.

Burt was riding far to the west, and he had no coat or poncho of any kind tied behind his saddle. But he was in no mood to hurry home. He wanted to watch the coming miracle.

The big drops started to fall and then the whole heavens suddenly seemed to open wide. He pulled Sleepy Red down to a walk and took off his hat. He wanted to shout like a Holy Roller. It was a visitation—a holy manifestation.

Nothing in his life had ever felt as good as this rain pelting down on his bare head. He wished that he'd taken off his shirt so that it might seep inside him.

Sleepy Red turned slowly toward the ranch. The cows they passed did not look so thin and pathetic, nor did they bawl out their reproaches to him.

And the creeks that had been dry for so long made music once again as the yellow and brown and red floods rolled down their pinched bosoms. They, too, were happy, and suddenly life itself was full and beautiful.

He'd have a chance now. Maybe he could still keep going and he wouldn't forever be marked a failure.

If these rains would only keep up, there'd be summer grass and fall browse. He could winter the remaining stuff here and maybe the ranch could keep alive. It was little short of magic what a few good rains could do to this Southwest country.

He was so happy he could have danced a jig. The ranch still might be saved. He hurried a letter off to Pueblo begging the owners to hold on a little longer.

He counted the days till he got an answer. They were glad to get the news of the breaking of the drouth, they wrote, but Burt was to go ahead with the plans for cleaning up the outfit. He should sell the stuff he still had at Rhodes Spring and he was to try to get an offer for the buildings and ranch site, and the few acres of irrigated hay land.

Burt knew that it was the verdict from which there was no appeal. He was done.

He arranged to ship out the two trainloads of stuff at the spring. They were in excellent shape and the only satisfaction he had from his six long hard years of work was that this big gamble against orders paid off big. The owners had not criticized him when he had first written about what he'd done, but they had made little comment.

A buyer paid him $24 the round for the herd he drove across the *Jornada* to the shipping yards at Engle. It was the top price for New Mexico cattle for that last year of the great dry-up.

Burt combed the country for buyers for the ranch buildings and the irrigated pasture and the good-will of the Bar A Bar. But the district was strapped, and even faith in cattle was broken.

But Burt knew that this range and this unique and thrilling business would someday come back into its own. He still had plenty of faith in the long pull. It didn't make good sense to him to quit now. He wanted to stay on and show what he could do, if he only had a fair break of luck. He still was willing to fight on against those ancient twin enemies—bad weather and low prices.

He had saved his wages, and made a little money on a long-shot mine gamble, and before the dry-up ruined everything he'd gathered in a few dollars from buying odd calves and yearlings that his Mexican neighbors had raised and could not keep. He'd lump it all together and make an offer for the physical properties of the Bar A Bar. He figured $3,000 was fair, especially when he hadn't been able to get a single outside bid.

The company wired their acceptance, and Burt now owned his own ranch. He started out to raise money to partly restock it. But it was in the early spring of 1893, and the Cleveland Panic was on. Money was tighter than the bark on a tree, and he couldn't borrow enough to buy even a hundred head of skinny, bawling yearlings.

-- *8* --

Within a few weeks he had everything cleaned out and he nailed shut the door of his ranch house, packed his gear on the spare horse he owned, mounted Vic and headed up-river for San Marcial.

He had a little poker money in his pocket, and the distinct feeling that he'd be better off if he had that $3,000 in his hip

pocket rather than buried back there in the hills. Still, the whole country was broke, and he knew he wasn't any worse off than thousands of others. Maybe he was in the wrong business, but he sure didn't know anything but cows.

After he'd loafed around the railroad town for a couple of days F. J. Easley, the division superintendent and a friend of his, asked him what he was figuring on doing.

"Well, right now I been thinking on holding up a Santa Fé passenger train," Burt answered.

"Maybe I could give you a job; my head bookkeeper has just quit. I could pay you $120 a month."

"Mister, you just hired yourself a bookkeeper," Burt said, with a broad grin.

Burt managed to get along fine, but he wasn't cut out for desk work. After a few months he struck the boss for a pass to the Chicago World's Fair. He was told that an employee didn't rate a pass until he'd been with the company for a year.

Burt waited until Easley had gone to El Paso, and then he wrote himself a pass, packed the valise he had bought that first time he'd ridden in a caboose to Dodge, and took the night train. It was the first time he'd ever been in the Windy City, and it was his first World's Fair.

He had been in town a week when he drifted over to the stockyards and into the offices of the commission firm of Clay & Robinson, and was handed a letter. Burt had left word back in New Mexico that this would be his forwarding address.

The letter was signed by Frank C. Bloom, cattleman and banker of Trinidad, Colorado, and it had been written on Palmer House stationery several days before. Burt was to call at the hotel for a conference about a matter that might prove mutually advantageous. Burt hurried downtown but the clerk at the Palmer House said Mr. Bloom had left four days previously.

Burt was finished with hootchy-kootchy dancers and the Midway sights, so he left on the first train going west. Three days later he called on Mr. Bloom at his office in the bank in Trinidad, where he was first vice-president.

Mr. Bloom had a reddish brown beard and kindly hazel eyes, and Burt knew he was honest. He was in partnership in the cattle business with his brother-in-law, Mahlon Thatcher, and a younger Thatcher brother, who were bankers in Pueblo. Maybe Burt had better take the train north to confer directly with the senior Thatcher. The banker-rancher in Pueblo explained that he had heard that Burt had done a fine job cleaning up a New Mexico ranch for the Lankford Brothers, who lived only a few blocks down the street from the Thatcher residence.

Burt could hardly believe his ears. He had not really failed, after all, despite the complete victory of those two old mortal enemies. He'd done his level best. The ranch had failed, but not Burt. He was actually being offered a bigger job than he'd ever had.

Bloom and the Thatchers were financially interested in some ten or twelve thousand head of cattle scattered over a rough country along the Verde River in the Bloody Basin, north of Phoenix, Arizona. The three men owning the outfit were heavily indebted to the bankers, and for the past nine years the ranch manager hadn't been able to trail enough beef out of the inaccessible Basin to meet even the interest charges. The backers wanted to get at least part of their bait, cut their losses and call it quits. At best it was a disheartening proposition for any outsider to face.

Mr. Thatcher was frank and straightforward. He warned Burt that it was a hard, murderous land, without roads or even good trails. On to the east, across the rugged Mazatzals, lay the misnamed Pleasant Valley, that had been the scene of the terrible Graham-Tewkesbury feud.

To the northeast above the Verde River range stretched the great Hash Knife outfit, with its 60,000 head of cattle, and its unsavory reputation of having "the thievinist, fightinist" bunch of cowboys in the United States. Any man who undertook the task of cleaning out the wild stuff from the Bloody Basin would need plenty of guts, patience and luck.

Burt didn't hesitate. He said he'd be glad to try it.

It would give him a chance to show what he could really do. He'd had two strikes on him all those years he'd been at the Bar A Bar—bad weather and low prices. And he'd been young and inexperienced.

He'd have rough sledding on this Arizona job, too. But he was twenty-six now, and as long as he was dealing with cattle he wasn't afraid to tackle it. A man learned in this world.

And maybe things would break better for him this time.

Part Two

Ranch Manager

BURT realized what he was up against before he was half-way through his inspection trip over the Bloody Basin.

He had never seen such violent, difficult country, and the prospect of gathering, holding and then trailing out the thousands of head of wild cattle ranging back in these canyons, wooded slopes and distant valleys, appalled him.

He found the three owners, Granville Graybeal, D. L. Murray and Walter Hudson, all friendly men and agreeable to matching their ranch holdings against their indebtedness to the Thatchers and Bloom. They had had more than enough of trouble during the past nine years. And now in the late fall of 1893 cattle prices were as low as they had been since the late '60's when the great Texas breeding grounds started their living streams of cattle flowing to the fattening ranges of the north.

Granville Graybeal, who had once run a dairy in Pueblo, was the active manager of the outfit. He was a bachelor, about forty, and spent most of his time at the headquarters cabin far up the Verde River. Burt liked his frankness and honesty.

"The trick is to get the big stuff out," he explained, with a shake of his head. "That's what busted us."

The two men rode north from Phoenix at sun-up on a bright Monday morning. Eight miles out of the city they watered their animals and filled their canteens in the Arizona Canal. It was forty-five miles before they'd hit water again on Camp Creek.

On north, straight in front of them, stretched the sandy wastes of Paradise Valley. Giant cholla cactus raised their heads high above the lowly cat's-claw, mesquite and ironwood.

"Those cholla are the villains," Granville pronounced with considerable bitterness. "Every time we've tried to bring a trail herd down through here, they've defeated us. Their fishhook barbs just seem to jump at a steer's tail. One swish and the brute has needled himself from hell to breakfast—and away he goes! All the cowboys in Arizona couldn't hold them after that."

Time and again, he explained, he'd tried this short southern desert route, but always the big stuff would stampede on him. Half of them would break back to the distant hills and deep canyons of the Bloody Basin. The best he'd been able to do in recent years was to bring out little batches of three or four hundred yearlings or mixed stock cattle at a time. Oddly enough, cows and calves seemed to quiet down a herd.

"Can't you trail out on west to Prescott, or go straight up north to Flagstaff?" Burt asked.

"Wait'll you see the country," Granville answered, with a shake of his head. "You can hardly get a packmule in or out of the Basin except through this desert."

It was getting dark when the two men struck water. They spent that night at Camp Creek and at daybreak climbed up a steep six-mile incline and then dropped down to the Verde. As they moved on north the country grew wilder, and Burt began to wonder how a man could drive the company's four-mule team and heavy wagon over the deep ruts and heavy rocks, and up and down the steep grades.

Some twenty miles on upstream they reached a long, one-story building that was called Camp Supply. It was the end of the wagon road, and the four-mule outfit was kept busy a good part of the year bringing up rolled barley and general ranch supplies and storing them here. Horses working the round-ups had to be grained or they wouldn't have a chance against the aged, fleet cattle in the rough country.

Eight or ten big mules and a batch of tough burros, in charge of a packer and his helper, packed the stuff from Camp Supply on up the twenty-mile trail to headquarters.

Burt and Granville reached the log cabin with its pole lean-to late that afternoon. The four cowboys who were the year-round hands rode in shortly after they arrived. The head rider was a level-headed, soft-spoken Texan named Hayden Justice. Burt was sure satisfied with his looks. The boys were busy rebuilding pole catch-corrals and packing salt, for the fall round-up was scheduled to start in a couple of weeks.

Granville offered to show Burt over the whole Bar 0 0 range. Burt said he wouldn't bother him but that he'd be grateful if he'd send him out a round-up cook and three or four more riders when he got back to Phoenix.

"I'll pick 'em up for you at Tempe," Granville promised.

The next morning Burt and Hayden Justice rode east across the Verde, and on up the rough East Fork, and then over high, timber-covered slopes and ridges until they reached the divide of the Mazatzals. On to the east stretched the great Tonto Basin, where the Grahams and Tewkesburys had feuded to the last man.

Burt was glad of this chance to look over the range and the cattle, and he kept his eye peeled for a new trail out of the Basin. He was about convinced that he'd have to turn to the western side when the great barrier of the Mogollon Rim suddenly loomed up in front of him. He threw up his hands. The Rim was a veritable stone wall, a thousand feet high, apparently blocking all hopes of reaching Flagstaff and the railroad.

Two days later he and Hayden rode west of the Verde as far as the Big Bug. The head rider described the nature of the country on northwest to the Santa Fé railhead at Del Rio, half-way between Ash Fork and Prescott. Among other difficulties there'd be a forty- or fifty-mile dry drive, Hayden explained.

"Let's try it," Burt solemnly pronounced. He liked and trusted this narrow-hipped cowboy, who reminded him so much of Charlie Wall and Warren Carpenter. But he couldn't understand why the old management hadn't broken the trail.

"Them farmers couldn't drive a bunch of milk cows down a fenced lane," Hayden answered. "I'll bet we can make it, boss."

Back at headquarters Burt looked over the riding stock he had inherited. There were some forty excellent mountain horses, chunky, short-coupled animals with good feet and strong hearts. Hayden pointed out a brown riding mule named Daisy, and pronounced her the best mountain animal in the remuda. She had a black mate named Bessie, whom he claimed was almost as good as Daisy.

The horses and the riding jennies had to be shod all the way around. Burt teamed up with Hayden, and in one day the two fitted and nailed on forty-four Burden shoes. Great care had to be used that the iron calks of the front shoes did not stick out behind the hoofs, where they might be tramped on by the front tip of a hind shoe. A man's life often depended on his horse being properly shod.

-- 2 --

The night chill of the high places was still in the dawn air on the late fall day when the pack outfit and the men and remuda started out from the cabin and, single-file, headed north up the Verde. Each man had a string of three grain-fed horses, and two of the boys had either Daisy or Bessie as one of their mounts.

Three big packmules carried the bedrolls, and the cook had his pots and pans and grub tied down on a trio of burros. The packer closed up the rear of the column with his eight mules loaded down with heavy burlap sacks of rolled barley.

They made camp in a flat valley that had a small creek cutting down its middle. At daybreak Burt led his eight men off to the right and up a series of steep rocky hills. They dropped off one at a time and when the quarter-circle net was completed each man was on his own.

They were after beef, but that took in everything that was two years old or better, including dry cows. The calves had been branded back in June.

It was wild, dangerous work. A man would catch sight of a big-horned critter, and take after it on the dead run. If the beast chose to high-tail it down a rocky, gullied mountainside the man and horse had no choice but to follow at the dead run. When the rider could keep the critter headed for the round-up grounds he was playing in luck. Two or three men stayed below to hold up the wild stuff as they'd come piling down the steep slopes.

That first night the gather was eased into a corral, and the men got a good sleep. For two days the same round-up grounds was used, then the little herd was moved on down the canyon and a new camp and holding ground laid out. Men had to day-circle and night-herd the catch from here on.

Once a small herd had been brought together and broken to trail, it was easier to hold the wild additions. But there was constant trouble. The old mossy horns would wait their chance, and quick as a flash they would break out of the herd and race for the rocks and gorges they had just left.

Often the men would tie a wild critter to the horns of a fairly tame animal, until the fight and the urge to escape had left him. There was little use trying to be humane with the big, aged brutes. Many of the old steers and bulls were as dangerous as grizzly bears, and they would fight until they played out from sheer exhaustion.

Burt did his full share and more. He had never seen such reckless cowboying, but it pleased him. A man had to pull up the cinch of his saddle and tighten the strings of his own nerves each time he took after one of the big fellows. Death lurked on every stony hillside and canyon wall. Many of the older critters had been defying capture for years, and hundreds had neither been branded nor castrated and their horns were long and sharp.

But the danger and excitement suited Burt. There was something primal and deeply satisfying about roaring down a rocky slope after a thousand-pound steer. It took a man with *cahones grandes* to drop his rope over a big brute's horns and then bust him wide open. It was a hundred times more dangerous than ordinary roping, and the thrill it gave a rider lifted him into the realm of pure exaltation.

Burt reveled in his own accomplishments. He had two big Mexican vaqueros who didn't even know the word fear, and he determined to keep up with them. They had a cruelty he lacked, but he asked no odds when it came to dangerous riding, roping and tying down.

Each man carried a small saw-blade tied under the leather skirts of his saddle, so that he could saw off the tips of the horns of the wilder critters. When they'd finished this operation, the two Mexicans would cut the cord just over the steer's knee-cap, so that the animal would never be able to run again.

Burt's own favorite method of taming an old battler was to cut two holes in an empty barley sack and then pull it down over his horns. The steer could only see the ground at his feet. Then he would haze the animal to the gathered herd, and usually the aged reprobate would seek the center of the circle and stay there. Several times Burt ordered his men to stop sewing up the eyelids of the worst of the critters. It was too cruel to suit him.

For long, hard days the men worked the rough country, up and down the canyons of the Verde. Men were badly bruised and cut, muscles strained and joints sprained, and clothes torn to rags, despite the heavy leather chaps. But the little herd grew, and in less than a month it numbered around a thousand head.

It seemed a wise thing to stop the round-up and make the try of trailing out the big stuff that was now gathered. Burt wanted to make this first trail herd at least fifteen hundred head of beef, but he knew that every day he delayed he ran the chances of a stampede and a breaking back into the hills of all the wild stuff they had worked so hard to get down. Men and horses were almost exhausted by the additional work of standing day and night guard over the gather.

Many of the hoofs of the tougher, older animals were worn down to the bone. It was pitiful to see the limping, suffering veterans plodding down the rocky trail toward the big flat that Burt had picked out for a final holding ground.

There was nothing to do but cut back the critters with the worst hoofs. They would never be able to keep up with the herd on the terrible drive that lay ahead. What was needed was a rest of two or three weeks to let the cattle recuperate, but that couldn't be done in this open mesa.

At the western end the flat narrowed and Burt posted Hayden opposite him, with a man on each side. Then he had the herd trailed out and slowly moved between him and Hayden. As each hundredth critter would go by Burt would shout "Count!" and tie a knot in the string he held. Each made it exactly one thousand and eight head.

The trail drive, accustomed now to day and night herding, moved out quietly. The second afternoon they hit Bug Creek and followed it until dark, when the cattle were bedded down on a rough flat back from the stream. The whole country looked as if it were cut into strips of steep arroyas and dangerous washes, and Burt was worried. There was a spooky feeling in the air.

He had every man tie up a night horse, and he assigned half the men to ride circle, with the relief coming out at midnight. The change in the night shift had barely been made when the first bolt of lightning ripped through the black night. The big steers already on their feet were off before the second flash cut across the sky.

Burt and Hayden had been with the first shift, and when they stretched out on their tarp for a little sleep each held the reins of his night horse in his hands. At the first crash of lightning they jumped for their ponies.

It was pitch dark and the footing was dangerous, but the two men raced toward the sound of the running cattle. In some

strange manner the herd, on its own accord, broke into several
bunches, and the two top riders separated.

It was difficult to turn the leaders of the several batches and
for what seemed miles each man raced alongside his hold. Burt
gave his horse his head, and several times he was conscious of his
pony leaping over dry washes that he could not see and that
might have meant death to them both.

When dawn broke he found that he was holding some five
hundred exhausted cattle. Slowly he trailed them back toward
camp. At one steep-banked gully he counted ten head flounder-
ing about with broken legs. He would come back with his rifle
and end their misery.

The riders began to dribble in, each man driving the few
head he had rounded up. An hour later Hayden showed up with
two or three hundred. When all the men were accounted for
and they had breakfast, Burt had the cattle strung out for a fresh
count. They were out exactly thirty head. Burt figured that maybe
the only real loss was the ten that had piled up in the arroyo.
The other twenty probably had headed back for the hills of home.

Late that afternoon Burt had the cattle thrown into a tight
circle and a double guard posted. At dawn they would leave the
Bug and start the forty-mile waterless drive across Lonesome
Valley.

The men fed themselves and their horses in the dark, and
only a suspicion of light was breaking out in the east when they
began the long, dry drive. If the cattle had been in good shape
the forty-odd miles could have been covered nicely in two days,
but there were too many sore-footed brutes to figure on pushing
through that fast.

At noon the following day, when the herd was checked and
the men ate their cold biscuit and chunks of meat, Burt suddenly
changed his mind and decided to try to reach water that night.

A rough, twelve-mile downgrade lay ahead. At the bottom

and cutting across the trail flowed a living stream, as broad and almost as deep as a "mother" irrigation ditch. Before the cattle had covered half the distance Burt posted riders ahead of the leaders.

Suddenly an old mossy horn lifted his head and sniffed the air. He bellowed and struck out at a lumbering trot. Others followed. They could smell the water that awaited them six miles farther on.

The men swung their ropes and ponchos in the faces of the crazed cattle, and yelled until they were hoarse. For a time they managed to slow down the leaders, but when there was a mile or two still to go Burt waved the men aside. When the stronger animals reached the creek, the herd was spread out for more than a mile.

That night the cattle were quiet, and for two days they were held on grass along the stream while Burt rode ahead the few miles to the railhead at Del Rio and ordered two trains. He would go with the first train with one of the boys, and send Hayden and another man with the second. He had orders to ship to a siding called Thatcher near Pueblo and put the cattle on company grass.

Burt was completely tired out. He'd made it, but it had been an exhausting experience. The cattle were gaunt and many of them had lost as much as a hundred pounds. He was positive now of two things. First, he must locate and fence a big pasture, where he could hold the foot-sore steers that were gathered until they were in shape to start for the railroad.

And then he must find another way out of the Basin.

-- 3 --

Burt had his eye on a valley that was roughly six miles square. On two sides were sharp hills and cut-banks, ribboned with deep ravines and dry gullies.

He figured that by stopping up the rocky draws with cedar poles, and then stringing barbed wire across the two ends, he could have a tight holding pasture that would be almost as big as a township. The western end narrowed down to less than two miles, and a stream cut through the center.

He rode south to Phoenix, and shortly he had his wagon packing up the wire and staples to run a four-wire fence. His pack-train was assigned to bringing the stuff on from Camp Supply, while his men cut cedar posts from the timbered slopes that half surrounded the pocket.

While he was fencing the Big Pasture, he made several exploring trips in the hope of finding a better way out for the cattle. Riding off to the northeast with Hayden one morning, they made their way up and down canyons and steep rimrocks to the cabin of an eccentric ex-Confederate soldier, called Old Hutch. The odd character ran some thirty mares, and raised and broke mountain horses. At this time the Territory was paying a bounty of twenty dollars for the scalps of mountain lions, and Old Hutch did considerable hunting.

The cabin was perched on a high mesa, and there was no one at home when Burt and Hayden drew up. It was well after two, and they had had no dinner.

They entered the cabin and found a pan of stew simmering on a bed of live coals in the corner fireplace. On a littered table was a plate of hard soda biscuit. The whole place was dirty and unswept, but the visitors helped themselves to the food and enjoyed their lunch. The stew tasted like tender meat from a yearling, and Burt grinned when he wondered if he was not eating his own beef.

On their way down the opposite side of the ridge, they ran into Old Hutch at work in a small irrigated plot of ground. His beard was long and matted, and his clothes were as crudely patched as Joseph's coat. Hayden knew him and introduced him to his boss.

"Wal, you fellers ride on back to the cabin and I'll git you somethin' to eat," he drawled, scratching his gray beard with his dirty fingers.

"Thanks," Burt said, "but we helped ourselves to that stew of yours."

"Good God!" Old Hutch exclaimed.

"It was good, too," Burt added.

"Say! That was a panther I killed yestiddy. I was cookin' it up fer my dogs."

Hayden slid down from his horse and stepped over behind a cat's-claw bush. He was a hard man, but his stomach apparently was easily upset.

Burt and Hayden next turned to the east side of the Verde in their search for another way out of the Basin. Over to the north it was even rougher and wilder. Like explorers touched with some half-mad zeal they rode on and on.

On this second venture they took along a packmule and Burt swore he would not turn back until they had found and marked out a new trail. He led Hayden into country his head rider never knew existed. Often they'd have to back-track to get out of a deep box-canyon, or off a high mesa that had sheer cliffs a hundred feet high.

Finally they could see the great Mogollon Rim looming ahead and trailing far off to the eastward toward Apache land. It was a challenge, an affront, a dare to the stubborn Burt. Like the crack of a pistol he sprung the proposition of leading a herd straight up over the Rim.

Hayden drew in a deep breath and the crow's-feet around his gray eyes fairly cracked. "You're the boss," he slowly said. "We can shore try her."

Burt had made his play and he meant to stick to it. He was relieved and happy. He had a goal now that would be well worth the fight it would take to gain it.

His brother Thad, eleven years his junior, had written that he'd like to join Burt at the Basin. He'd tell him to come on and see the fun.

With the letter went the ticket money. For almost ten years now he'd been sending money home. When he left the Monticello outfit he bought the best team and wagon the ranch had and got a man to drive it to his father's place. He'd sent Dana to college for two terms and he was now arranging for his sister to go to school in Iowa. And never a month went by that he didn't write his mother an affectionate letter. Usually there was a yellow-back enclosed.

When Thad arrived Burt was surprised to see how big and strong he was for seventeen. Before long he grew a full blonde beard, and the boys got to calling him "Mormon Bishop."

Thad seemed to enjoy fighting and Burt suddenly realized that he himself had been the same sort of a kid. He'd learned to control his temper and accept responsibility the hard way. That was a part of growing up.

Thad had worked on one or two New Mexico ranches and he was a good roper. Burt assigned him the brown mule Daisy, and he took considerable pride in the way the boy and the little jenny tied into the big stuff.

But he had Hayden keep an eye on the kid so he wouldn't bite off more than he could chew. It was mighty easy to get killed in this wild country.

-- 4 --

The second round-up was well along when Burt spied an old mossy horn in a rough patch of scrub cedar that clung with a grip of death to the rocky slope of a hillside. He had his coiled rope in his left hand, alongside his reins, while the loop hung ready in his right hand. Here in this dangerous country even the Texans did not tie hard-and-fast, but dallied around their saddle horns so they could turn a critter loose if they got in a jackpot.

Burt was riding a fine roping horse named Snort, and he jabbed in the spurs and went after the steer, hell-bent for election. The big fellow broke for the open, then dodged back into a patch of pines. In and out, up and down, he led the chase. Just about the time horse and man and steer were all three pooped out, the critter half-slid down the slope to where it debouched into a rough flat, with a spring over to one side. Burt managed to make his catch and flip the rope over the steer's side, then taking a quick dally he turned Snort to the left and busted the old mossy horn with a bang. In a matter of seconds he had him cross-hobbled, his piggin' string tied fast from a front foot to the opposite foot behind. Then for good measure he tied together the front feet.

Burt stumbled over to a big rock, and cursed slowly and fervently. He was mad clean through. Snort stood with head down, breathing deeply while the sweat rolled from his heaving sides. This ornery critter had pretty near caused the death of both of them.

After a good rest, Burt stepped up and rode off. Mister Steer could lie there for the night and think things over.

The next morning he rode in and slipped off the rope that tied the front legs together, but he left on the cross-hobble. Then he prodded the critter to his feet. The animal glared at him, hate smoldering in his eyes.

Burt hit him across the rump with the hondo of his rope, but he would not budge.

He hit him again. The mossy horn bawled, and swung his vicious horns as if he would take to him. But he did not budge.

Yet Burt knew he was half-dead from thirst, and there was water less than a hundred yards away.

Burt rode off. The next morning when he returned, the steer was lying down. Again he got him to his feet, but again he failed to drive him to the spring.

The third morning Burt came back with a little batch of tame cattle. He cut the hobbles, but the steer wouldn't even get up. He would look up at Burt with hate showing in his blood-shot eyes. He was weak and dying of thirst, but he would not budge.

Burt got down and twisted his tail. He tried every means he knew of to get him to his feet. But the animal willed to die.

Three mornings later when Burt rode in, the old warrior was dead. He had not given in to man. He had been captured but he had not been vanquished.

Burt couldn't help but be touched by the dumb brute's stubborn hate and his inner courage. This time it was man who had been defeated.

Things were a lot easier this year, with the Big Pasture to fall back on. As soon as he'd get a batch of a hundred or so gathered, Burt would drive them to the permanent holding grounds. There was plenty of grass and water there, and it was working like a charm when it came to healing the sore hoofs.

By the end of June he figured he had gathered as big a herd as it was safe to handle in one trail herd. There was silent disapproval among most of the men when Burt announced that he would point the drive straight up the East Fork of the Verde, and cross the deep canyons of Strawberry and Fossil Creeks. Then he'd lead them up over the Mogollon Rim, and on across the high mesa to Clear Creek and on to Flagstaff. The cowboys whispered among themselves that the new boss must be touched by the altitude.

In 1875 General George Crook had built a Military Road from the little-used army post of Camp Verde on southwest to Payson. By far the most difficult stretch was a narrow wagon trail that he had hacked, foot by foot, up the rocky slope of the Rim. It had been used very little, and for a number of years now it had been abandoned. The flash rains had cut deep gullies across it and dug out chunks of the rock bed, until the Rim Road was all but impassable, even for a man on horseback. Burt knew the risks he was running, but he was going to tackle that Rim come hell or high water.

His count was 1770 head on the morning he started out from the Big Pasture. Soon he was breaking trail through a fearsome land. At times he pointed the herd along the side of canyons so steep that the midday sun could barely reach the dancing stream two thousand feet below. Often he was forced to lead the cattle down rocky slopes to water, and then fight his way up the opposite banks.

His men grew quarrelsome and short-tempered, and there were constant bickerings and fights. His kid brother Thad actually seemed to enjoy the daily brawls as much as he did his meals. Burt played no favorites.

Day and night he was in the saddle, keeping his men awake and working, wearing out his mounts, doing double turn at night guard-tireless, indestructible, omnipresent. His will never weakened, and he drove his body with a stern, quiet fury.

The third night out he tried to hold the herd on a bed ground half-way up the slope of a canyon wall. Shortly after darkness the cattle broke and went thundering down the dangerous incline.

But Burt had outthought them. Just before twilight he had sent two men with axes to a spot down the creek bottom where the canyon narrowed. His roving eyes had noted the narrows, and also the fact that cottonwoods had, by some miracle, gained a foothold here in the rocks.

"Cut down enough trees to bottle up the trail," he had ordered. "Then if these damn doggies want to stampede, let 'em!"

The barricade stopped the wild, frightened cattle, but it was a hideous night. All that next day he held them there, while they quieted down. At dawn on the second morning he led the way out of the river bed to a high mesa, and then cut on northeast along Strawberry Creek, in the direction of the little Mormon settlement of Pine.

Turning due north, they followed the deep canyon of Fossil Creek to a point where they could look up at the Mogollon Rim, cutting directly across their path. They were now at the foot of the abandoned Military Road that led up the side of the Rim.

Like a giant snake the trail twisted and wound its way up the long, tortuous slope. At times it would disappear from the view of those standing at its base. To the eye, the Rim looked as impregnable and forbidding as the high walls of an ancient citadel.

Burt sliced off thirty head of big steers, and with a man ahead and the trusted Hayden behind started the little batch on the great adventure. They trailed out single file, and Burt eagerly watched the line wind up the uncertain path hacked out of the side of the Rim, until it passed out of sight. It was a terrific gamble he was taking. He was betting seventeen hundred head of cattle against a hunch. Five minutes after the first bunch had left, he started up a second group, with no rider in front but with a seasoned man behind. There must be no crowding and the steers must set their own pace. He knew that Hayden and his helper would locate a good holding ground—if and when they reached the top of the Rim.

When he had started up the sixth batch, and had only a single man remaining behind with him, he called a halt until the riders could return. He had told Hayden to keep one boy to help him hold the herd at the top of the Rim, and not to let the other riders start down until the sixth bunch of cattle arrived.

The minutes dragged by for Burt and the boy waiting below. Finally they caught sight of a rider coming slowly around a curve high up on the trail. Five men were following him. Burt knew his hunch had paid off.

The boys had strange tales to tell of the terrible Rim Road. At times the cattle, traveling single file, had to hug the inside of the rocky trail while they picked their way around great boulders and across dangerous washouts.

All day long Burt sent out his little batches of cattle, moving a total of two hundred head on each journey. It was twilight when the last critter took to the Rim Road, and he motioned to the horse wrangler to lead off with his remuda. Early in the afternoon he had sent up the cook and his pack outfit.

Hayden was holding the big herd a mile or two back from the lip of the Rim, in a wide draw with a creek in its bottom. The worst was over. They had conquered the Rim.

-- 5 --

But ahead lay a fifty-mile dry drive through rough country splotched with patches of cedar and hemlock. It was a high land and while it had no deep canyons or tough mountains, it was difficult to take cattle through.

Burt and Hayden criss-crossed the country ahead, one on each side of the trail herd, searching for water-holes and springs. The second day they located enough water off to the east to take care of the horses and mules. Burt ordered that the dregs be held back, and when the main herd, already half-crazed from thirst, was well ahead he trailed the forty head or so of weakened, sore-footed animals to water.

The nights were unbelievably cool and sharp, and as long as there was sufficient light Burt kept the herd moving. It was around four the afternoon of the third day when the tough old steers in the vanguard caught their first whiff of water. A tiny breeze was blowing from the north, and it carried with it the promise that set the hearts of these weary, thirst-mad cattle beating high.

Burt knew that five miles on ahead lay the great Mormon

Lake, and he made little effort to hold back the herd. When he finally reached the lake with the dregs, he pushed back his hat and grinned happily at the sight of the big critters standing belly-deep in the cool waters.

There was a little grass on the slopes stretching away from the lake, and he decided to let the cattle loiter here for a day. Half the time they would quietly graze and then they would walk slowly into the water and stand there contentedly chewing their cuds.

Burt instructed Hayden to move the herd on the second day the dozen miles or so on north to the center of Clark's Valley, and hold them there while he jogged it to Flagstaff and ordered the stock trains. There was plenty of water and grass in the valley, and it would be good for the beef after this hard, grueling drive.

Burt came back with bad news. A railroad strike was on and there was no freight moving either way out of Flagstaff. They'd have to hold the cattle and take things easy. A little later when the beef herd had fully settled down the men could take turns twisting the monkey's tail in Flagstaff, ten miles on north.

When the strike started there was a carload of oranges in the freight train that had pulled in at a siding. The oranges were spoiling and an enterprising merchant had bought them for a song by telegraph, and was selling them at 50 cents a crate. Burt hired a pack mule and brought out four crates, and each boy could eat more oranges than he'd had in all his life.

The second day they staged a ball game with the precious fruit, but it quickly degenerated into a battle royal. When it was over, most of two full crates had been used up. Burt was plenty disgusted. He bluntly told the boys he'd see 'em all frying in hell before he ever bought them another orange.

On that first visit to Flagstaff Burt arranged with a local bank to honor his checks. He knew the boys would want the money coming to them when they rode into town. The result was plenty of big heads, but the only man who gave him any trouble was old Jim, the cook.

At best he was an evil-tempered, cantankerous cuss, but when he came back roaring drunk he was nothing short of a public menace. When he failed to pick a fight with the boys, he grabbed the iron rod that was part of his cooking equipment and went to work on his pots and pans. Then he bellowed his challenges and started for the men.

Burt slipped his six-shooter in the waistband of his trousers, and got to his feet. Apparently he'd have to pistol-whip this crazy cook to keep him from killing somebody.

Burt was still thirty feet or more away when one of his pet hands, a weazened, bow-legged little Texan named Mat Lee, rode up. A few months before this Mat had been bitten on the wrist by a hydrophobia skunk, and Hayden had hustled him down to Pete Latourette, the Frenchman down on Deadman Wash, who'd cured him by applying a magic "mad stone" that was supposed to be found only in the stomach of certain rare deer. Anyway, Mat didn't die.

Quite unconscious of what was going on here at the camp, Mat stepped down, unsaddled and slipped the bridle off his pony. He was dragging his saddle by its pommel with his left hand, and dangling his heavy, silver-mounted bridle in his right, when Jim spied him.

The drunken cook made a bee line for the unsuspecting and undersized Mat. He swore he'd tear him limb from limb. Finally Mat spotted him, staggering straight toward him and waving the murderous iron rod.

The little cowpoke waited until Jim was just the right distance away. Then he swung his bridle over his head and the heavy California bit caught the cook squarely alongside the temple. It knocked him as cold as a mackerel. Mat had not even dropped his saddle, and he walked on to his bedroll as if nothing had happened.

Burt pretty near broke a hamstring laughing.

The herd was held for a full month at Clark's Valley. By the time Burt rode in with the news that the strike was over and the stock cars were arriving, most of the stuff had put back the tallow they had lost.

Two days later the men cut out 550 head and started them for the shipping pens. That would make up a full trainload. Every two or three days after that they'd slice off around half a thousand head and ship out.

Things had worked out all right, despite all the hard luck they'd had. But Burt was cured of the Mogollon Rim business.

The Big Creek trail and the dry drive to Del Rio on the west side was plenty bad enough, but it was a boulevard compared to this East Fork, Fossil Creek, Rim route.

That was too much like driving a herd through hell with a million red devils making it extra tough for the trail boss.

-- 6 --

The summer of '96 Burt decided on his own authority to go right ahead and gather and ship out all the big stuff he could find. He'd stag the bulls so that the cows would have no more calves and could fatten up.

As a rule he rode out with the last trainload of each shipment, and almost invariably he visited the Thatchers in their homes in Pueblo. They were agreeably surprised at the speed he was catching on to city ways and manners. He was no longer the uninitiated wagon boss, with cow manure on the heels of his boots.

When he stepped off at Pueblo after the fifth shipment from the Basin, he explained bluntly to the owners that he was liquidating the last of the holdings as quickly as he could. There were still some 2,000 big, aged stuff in the back ranges, and he'd get to work on them as soon as fall came.

Burt was well satisfied with his future prospects despite the fact that he was quickly working himself out of a job. He wanted to finish up the Basin and get on with his life. He had plenty of things to look forward to.

He drank a little hard liquor, now and again, and occasionally smoked a cigar. He noted that most of the important leaders of the community did both. Phoenix was a Western frontier capital, and the lawyers, politicians, bankers, railroad men and big cattlemen all liked to gamble and belly-up to the bar.

Although he was fairly new to Arizona, he had powerful friends scattered over the Territory. Bucky O'Neill, editor of *Hoofs and Horns* and popular figure of Prescott, was one of them. And there were Colonel Bill Greene and Governor Murphy and Colonel Randolph, head of the Southern Pacific's vast interests in the Southwest, and a dozen others. They all liked to have the stocky, happy-go-lucky Burt Mossman around them. He could tell a good story and play an excellent game of poker, and he was smart as a whip.

He was a bit flabbergasted when Acting-Governor Akers wrote him that he was appointing him one of Arizona's two delegates-at-large to a great cattlemen's meeting in Salt Lake City. Burt dressed up in his best bib-and-tucker and traveled north on a pass. It was a historic convention and marked the birth of the American National Livestock Association. Burt never forgot the unique honor, and all his life was loyal to the powerful organization.

His second adventure into the world of big men and gay conventions was his trip to California and then to Ogden, Utah, with Charlie Shannon in Colonel Randolph's private car. Shannon was a brilliant Westerner who'd made a fortune in mining and now was thoroughly enjoying life around the Territorial capital. Partly through his influence Burt was appointed a fellow-delegate to an irrigation convention in Ogden. Burt knew nothing about irrigation save the little he had absorbed when he helped his father dig the big ditch from the Rio Grande. But he played a good game of poker and Colonel Randolph, who happened to be going to the Coast at the same time, invited them both to share his private car.

It was quite an eye-opener for the ranch manager. The rugged, dangerous life of the Bloody Basin seemed far away and long ago from the luxury and fun of this journey to the moon. But Burt took it all in his stride.

Since there was little or nothing for him to do on the ranch until it was time for the final fall round-up, Burt decided he'd see a little something of the west coast of Mexico. In Phoenix he had met and made friends with a very fine Mexican broker and business man who lived in the seaport of Mazatlan, Sinaloa, some seven or eight hundred miles down the west coast. Burt was proud to introduce him to the Governor and Colonel Randolph and a number of his friends, and Señor Gonzales was touched by his kindness. In return he urged Burt to pay him a visit, explaining that he could travel by railroad from Nogales to Guaymas, and then take a comfortable coast boat on south to Mazatlan.

Burt had the time and the spare money, and he was anxious to see this little-known part of the coast country. When he arrived at Mazatlan Señor Gonzales welcomed him and more than reciprocated for the small favors Burt had shown him in Phoenix.

Among the several Americans at the port was the local manager of an American bank, and he and Burt were immediately taken with one another. At a lively drinking party one night, when Gonzales was not present, Burt seemed to rub a fat little captain of the Mexican army the wrong way. The captain, who was heavily loaded, made a loud speech denouncing the United States and its ability to fight any first-class power, including Mexico. There were other disparaging remarks and finally Burt reached over and slapped his face.

It was an insult no officer could stand, and the irate little captain promptly challenged Burt to a pistol duel. He demanded that it be fought at daybreak this very morning, and he named the spot and the terms. Each man would stand with his back to the other at fifteen paces. At the command they would turn and fire.

Burt had had a few drinks but he was by no means drunk, while his opponent was very much the worse for wear. It all seemed rather ridiculous to Burt but there was nothing for him to do but accept the challenge, since he had no idea of apologizing. A master of ceremonies was agreed on, and shortly after dawn broke the party left the café in cabs for their rendezvous with honor.

Burt figured out that his opponent obviously was too drunk to shoot straight, and that he'd wing him, but not kill him.

The cabs drew up at the edge of a park and the fifteen paces were stepped off, and the men took their places, their backs to one another. Burt drew his short-barreled .45 pocket Colt, while the captain had a German Luger. There was but one shot in each pistol.

The judge gave his final instruction and then stepped back.

"Tiran!" (Shoot!) he yelled.

The men whirled. The bullet from the Luger sung by Burt's left ear. He aimed high up at the officer's right side and the slug from his Colt tore through the shoulder-blade, spinning the victim in his tracks. It was a minor wound, exactly as Burt had planned it.

Suddenly a squad of local police appeared as if they had sprung out of the ground. Burt was grabbed and swished off to the jail and shoved into a filthy cell. A solid steel door closed shut behind him. The only light seeped in from a tiny barred window high up in the damp, stone wall. American friends found out about the affair and appealed to the U. S. Vice-Consul, who tried every way he knew to get Burt released, but he could do nothing.

For twenty-nine days Burt was held incommunicado. Once a day a plate of miserable food was pushed in through the slit in the steel door, while the jailer loosened a flood of abuse and insults on him. Every two or three days a pair of armed and uniformed guards stood by while there was a mock attempt at cleaning up the filth in his cell. No one laid a hand on him, but his pet jailer cursed and swore at him until Burt plotted to jump him and try to choke him to death, even if it cost him his own life.

He was sure that efforts were being made to secure his release, but he recalled tales he had heard of the terrible treatment given Gringos who had clashed with Mexican officials. He wished now that he had killed the fat captain, but he realized that he might have been beaten to death before he reached the jail.

The hideous nights and days snailed by. Burt studied the possibility of digging out through the thick wall, but when he had been thrown in the cell he had been searched and his money, watch, gun, penknife and every item he possessed had been taken from him. He was helpless but he still was not quite hopeless.

It was around ten one night when he heard a key inserted in the lock of his cell and then the steel door swung open. A Mexican with his hat pulled down low over his face whispered for him to come quickly and silently.

He followed him through the passageway. The outer steel door was open and on the floor nearby a man lay as if in a drugged stupor. In the flickering hall light Burt recognized him as the jailer who had been brutally abusing him. Burt turned back and kicked his tormentor until he was afraid he had broken his own toes.

In a moment he and his liberator were in the darkness of the alley outside the jail. Two horses with a man standing at their heads awaited them. He recognized the voice of his friend's son, the nineteen-year-old Eduardo Gonzales, when he whispered for him to mount quickly. The boy led the way on down the alley at a walk. The Mexican who had slipped him out of the prison disappeared into the night.

Thirty miles on north they found fresh horses, saddled and bridled, waiting for them at a small set of buildings off the main road. Three times in all they changed horses that night. It was well into daybreak when they pulled up at a cattle and goat ranch that lay three miles back from the coast. The two had ridden ninety miles.

For three weeks Burt lived quietly on the lovely little *hacienda* that had been in the Gonzales family for many years. He kept close to the main house and hid in his room at the approach of any visitor. The *peons* on the place loved the family and they proudly pledged their secrecy.

Early one night shortly after he had gone to bed, he heard the sound of a horse pounding down the trail from the sea. He was sure it would be good news for him.

One of Gonzales' *peons,* assigned to the task of keeping a beacon burning on a lonely point on the shore, slipped from his saddle and hurried to Burt with the word that a small boat from a steamer had come ashore and was waiting for him. A horse was hurriedly saddled and within a quarter-hour Burt had ridden the three miles to the sea and was being rowed to a ship standing a mile or two out, with no lights showing.

The Swedish captain of the little steamer met him at the Jacob's ladder and led him to his cabin. Burt apologized for the state of his clothes and the fact that he had no money to pay passage. The gruff old master smiled through his white beard as he handed him a roll of bills, explaining that it was a present from his friend Señor Gonzales of Mazatlan, who had hired him to drop anchor where the beacon burned, send a boat ashore and take him aboard. He was proceeding straight to San Pedro, the American port near Los Angeles.

When Burt turned in at the cabin that he shared with the

First Mate, he counted the roll of money. It was $300 in American bills. He swallowed a lump in his throat that he always swore was as big as the roll.

At Los Angeles Burt bought a new outfit of clothes and headed for San Francisco, where he had friends. His first task when he arrived there was to go to Shreve's Jewelry Store. He could draw on his own funds now and he bought a thousand-dollar diamond and had it set in a man's ring. Then he ordered it sent to Señor Gonzales through the American Vice-Consul at Mazatlan, who he knew had done his best to get him released.

(Fifteen years later, during a lull in the Mexican Revolution, Burt, recovering from an illness, had Colonel Randolph's private car at his disposal for a free trip on the recently completed Southern Pacific lines on down to Mazatlan and then south to Tepic. Burt invited several friends to go with him and he had the car lay over for a day at the port city where he had had his great adventure.

A cab drove him straight from the railway station to the home of his savior. A servant admitted him and a young man of thirty-four came forward to greet him. Burt failed to recognize him but his host gasped in happy astonishment and gave him the *abrazo* and kissed him on both cheeks.

"*Por Dios!*" he said. "Our dear friend—welcome to your house." Quickly he explained that his father had passed on several years before.

Burt had not missed at least one detail. On the finger of the young man's left hand was the great diamond he had sent his father from San Francisco.)

-- 7 --

Apparently the dueling adventure only whetted Burt's taste for more excitement, for he had not been back in Arizona more than a few weeks in this year of 1897, when he joined up with Alfred Donau in a cattle-buying expedition to the Yaqui River country in Sonora. Sonora was north of the Mexican State of Sinaloa, and since he'd be a good four hundred miles removed from his friend the jailer down in Mazatlan, he did not hesitate to make the trip.

His partner, Alfred Donau, was the young nephew of the powerful Albert Steinfeld, popular Tucson merchant and financier and president of the Consolidated Bank. Alfred had plenty of money back of him, and Burt had the knowledge and experience. It seemed a good idea for two young men to go in together and buy on speculation two or three trainloads of cattle.

The two young adventurers had a lot of fun working with a Mexican cattle buyer on down below the border, and in a very few weeks they had fourteen hundred two- and three-year-olds gathered and ready to ship. When the first trainload pulled out for the American border at Nogales, Burt and Alfred left the rest of the loading to their representative and took the passenger train north to Arizona.

Both were tired, dirty and hungry when they piled off the train and took a cab to the old Montezuma Hotel in Nogales. When they got cleaned up they back-tracked to the Mexican city of the same name. They would order a good dinner at a restaurant they knew and then they'd do the town.

Almost opposite the restaurant was a bar and gambling place. Alfred felt a lucky hunch.

"You go on in the café, Burt, and order dinner," he suggested. "I'll drop in here and touch up that monte game for enough to pay for a good meal."

Burt figured he had plenty of time after dinner to try his own luck, so he went ahead. He had the waiter hold back serving for a half-hour, then when Alfred did not show up he started eating. When he'd finished he paid for both meals and walked on across the street.

Alfred was in the red to the tune of four hundred dollars, and he was beginning to get a little worried. "Sit in here, Burt, and get my money back," he pleaded.

"I'm suspicious," Burt answered. "Don't tell me nothing; I'll bet on my own hunches."

When Alfred came back from eating, Burt had lost seven hundred dollars, and he was perspiring freely. He turned to Alfred.

"How far do you want to go in this partnership?" he questioned.

"As far as you want to take me," Alfred gamely answered.

Relieved and no longer embarrassed, Burt made a bet. When he finally pushed back his chair he had broken the bank. On the table in front of him was stacked three thousand two hundred dobie dollars—worth two for one U. S. dollar.

The partners paid a boy to get a wheelbarrow and a dozen small money sacks. They packed up their winnings and gaily trundled them through the customs and up to the old Montezuma Hotel. It was a barrel of fun to divide those two hundred pounds of shiny silver pesos.

The next day the stock trains came rumbling in and once again the two young gamblers made their split. Alfred was turning his half of the cattle onto one of his uncle's ranches. Burt had his seven hundred head shipped on up to Phoenix and in a few days W. J. Cotton had bought the lot for young Stanley McCormick of Chicago, at better than a two-dollar-a-head profit for Burt.

Neither of the boys succeeded in disposing of the bulk of their adobe winnings in the Nogales banks, so they carted their money bags on to Tucson. Burt ended up in Phoenix with his intact, and that night he arrived at the Palace Bar and sat himself down at the roulette table. While the wheel was still spinning he planked down two bags of silver on the red. On top of each bag he placed an American dollar. He won.

Old "Senator" Freeze casually counted out the Mexican dollars and paid off in American coin, one for two. It wasn't long until a crowd had gathered.

The sky was streaked with pinks and delicate rose shades when Burt called it a night. His bags of silver had melted away and he was as clean as a hound's tooth.

But he didn't mind in the least. He'd had a lot of fun and it really hadn't cost him a cent.

It was only free gravy he had spilled.

Burt ran into at least one interesting thing on his trip to the Yaqui River. Never had he seen men handle wild cattle like the Yaqui Indian cowboys down there. For his money they were the finest ropers and the best all-round vaqueros in the world.

Three or four of them who could talk fair Spanish had stuck with the cattle trains and ridden them on in to Phoenix. He hired them, along with a big, bruising half-Mexican, half-Yaqui, named Diego Bracamonte. Burt got him to round up two or three more of his stripe of Yaquis and half-breeds who were afraid of nothing that had hair on it.

Poor Hayden Justice had crossed over the big river. A year before, he had been stricken with virulent smallpox in Phoenix, and when he was recovering the doctor had warned him against overeating, particularly ice-cream. But Hayden went on a regular ice-cream jag. He died the next morning, just before daylight.

The drunken old cook, whom Mat Lee had tamed with the heavy California bit of his bridle that day up in Clark's Valley, also had checked out. He'd gone on a big drunk, and when the snakes started working on him he swallowed enough arsenic to kill a horse, and then shot himself through the temple for good measure.

The old crew was broken up, save only for his brother Thad and big "Dutch Charlie" Birkencamp. Charlie was a top hand, and he had a financial backer behind him.

Just before the final round-up started he offered Burt a straight ten dollars a head for everything that was still on the range. They estimated the left-overs at two thousand big animals, and Charlie posted a thousand dollars as earnest money.

For the twenty thousand dollars he was to get the cattle, range, cabins and good will—everything but the horses and mules. There would be no attempt at this time actually to gather and get out the big, aged stuff. But every animal was to be roped and tied down, and the count made by the men bringing in the top half of the right ear. Burt paid half the expenses, and agreed to put Charlie's mark on all unbranded critters, and castrate and dehorn all bulls gathered.

Burt dispatched a telegram to the Thatcher brothers at Pueblo. Mr. Frank Bloom, the partner from Trinidad, happened to be in Pueblo when the wire arrived.

The senior Thatcher slowly reread the wire: "Sold remnants estimated two thousand ten dollars head rope delivery." It made exactly ten words; Burt always was careful about spending company money.

"Now what in blazes does Mossman mean by 'rope delivery'?" the senior partner demanded.

"Damned if I know," the brown-bearded Mr. Bloom answered. "But if Burt says it, he'll do it."

Burt had coined a new word. In his private dictionary "rope delivery" simply meant that each animal would have to be roped and tied down, and a clip taken from the right ear. Every night the ears were to be brought in and carefully tallied by Burt and Dutch Charlie.

Burt led out his rip-snorting, ring-tailed bunch of Yaqui and Mexican vaqueros and turned them loose. They were as wild and untamed as the old mossy horns that they went after. Never in its life had the Bloody Basin seen such savage riding and violent competition.

Big Diego Bracamonte, his black eyes beady and shining, and his saddle-leather face glistening with sweat, was king of the wild bunch. It was food and drink to him to tie onto some great brute, with horns as sharp as cactus barbs, and race with him down a steep, rocky slope, where a misstep meant a broken leg or a broken neck.

The first afternoon when they were working Deadman Canyon, Burt watched him spur a man-killing bronc, that was pitching and squealing at every jump, straight down a hillside, with a thousand-pound bull on the end of his rawhide riata. By bit and spur, and wild will, he managed his untamed horse, and then mastered the bull.

And that night when the day's work was done, and the men were grouped around the cook's fire, Diego swaggered up to the little group. He was like some prehistoric figure as he pushed his great stubby fingers into the pockets of his leather chaps, and, one by one, pulled out his counters.

"*Uno!*" he shouted, flinging a hairy half-ear into the fire.

"*Dos!*" It was as if he were challenging his mates to question him.

"*Tres!*" He glared at his compadres as he bellowed the numbers.

"*Quatro! Cinco! Seis! Siete! Ocho!*"

He crashed his thick hands together to knock off the dirt. His flashing eyes swung from one Yaqui to another; from one half-breed border Mexican to the next. The echo of his roaring voice bounded back from the opposite wall of the canyon.

"Thar! You sonsabitches! Eight beeg wans! *Ocho!* Beat that, you *cabrons!*"

Dutch Charlie was no slouch himself. One evening as the men were hurrying back to camp and grub, they swept at a gallop down over a ridge into a draw filled with cat's-claw brush. In the bottom the men caught sight of a panther, crouching in the brush. The horses snorted and Diego's bronc came apart and "tried to chin the moon," as Everts Haley quotes Charlie Goodnight as saying. The rest of the horses followed suit, and in a second there was more Wild West than a man would see in a lifetime.

The horses got straightened out and took after the panther. They could see him claw his way up a big sycamore, close by the creek bed. Most of them had their ropes down by the time Dutch Charlie pulled up under the tree. He was riding a bay named Cuter, who weighed eleven hundred pounds and was all horse.

"Look out! He'll jump on you!" Burt yelled.

Charlie paid no attention, but built his loop and screamed at the big cat.

When it lit almost at the feet of his horse, Charlie dropped his noose and caught it around the neck. That instant it sprung on the horse and man, lighting squarely on Cuter's hindquarters.

One foot cut a great gash in the horse's flesh. The claws of the other foot ripped through Charlie's heavy leather chaps and his pants and underwear, but barely broke the skin.

Old Cuter came apart, and on the second jump the panther, with the rope still around his neck, loosened his hold and dropped off. Charlie socked in the steel, and the big bay bucked and plunged on down the dry, rocky creek bed.

Charlie held fast to his dally, but finally he let go his rope. Old Cuter calmed down. Back fifty feet or so the men found what was left of the panther. He had been beaten to death by the rocks Old Cuter had dragged him over.

He was an enemy with more aliases than an old-time badman: mountain lion—puma—cougar—panther. The blood and meat of yearling colts were his favorite, but his second choice was a fat calf.

Dogs ganged him and worried him until he gave up life; men poisoned him and shot him—and sometimes dragged him to death from the back of plunging, frightened horses. But as long as breath was in his body he was the wild, free agent hating and defying man.

Burt and his crew had roped, branded, sawed horns and cut off ears of a thousand head, when Dutch Charlie made a new proposition. He felt expenses were running too high, and although he was only paying half, he figured he would do better to take over the whole thing. Grass and water were his for the taking and he could gather at his leisure.

Burt figured there were probably eleven or twelve hundred head still hiding on the far edges of the Basin, but God alone knew how long it would take to get them out. So when Charlie offered him a flat ten thousand dollars for the remnants, he accepted the offer.

He settled on a fair price for the horses and mules and such equipment as the company owned. Charlie arranged for the payment, and Burt wired that the liquidation was complete.

Aside from his deal with Charlie, he had gathered and brought out from the Basin more than eight thousand head of stock not counting calves. And he had sold the wild bunch that remained for twenty thousand dollars. Thatcher Brothers & Bloom had their money back, with interest in full, and a clear profit of thirty-eight thousand dollars.

Burt got no bonus, but he'd done pretty fair. He'd established himself as a thoroughly competent ranch manager, ready and willing to tackle the most difficult cattle propositions. He had money in the bank, magnificent health and a host of friends.

He'd been loafing in the capital for a matter of two or three weeks when a letter came from a Mr. Ripley, president of the Aztec Land & Cattle Company, owners of the great Hash Knife outfit that ran on northeast of the Bloody Basin. Mr. Ripley was also Receiver of the Santa Fé Railroad and was a friend of the Thatchers.

The big cattle company was considering a change in management and would Mr. Mossman get in touch with G. L. Brooks, General Livestock Agent of the Santa Fé, whose headquarters were at Albuquerque, New Mexico?

Burt wired for an appointment and a meeting was arranged. Mr. Brooks wasted no time in offering him the job of superintendent of the mighty Hash Knife. The outfit owned outright 1,008,000 acres of railroad land, lying in alternate sections south of the Santa Fé tracks in northern Arizona. Its range ran for eighty miles west of Holbrook and forty miles to the south of the railroad. Every alternate section belonged to the U. S. government, but for all practical purposes it was Hash Knife range. That meant the ranch spread over more than two million acres.

For fourteen years the outfit had paid no dividends on either stock or bonds, but it had won the unsavory reputation of harboring more outlaw cowboys, more thieving hands and murderous neighbors, than any ranch in the country. Rustlers and horse thieves were as thick as fleas on a dog's back. It still ran around fifty thousand head of cattle and a couple thousand horses.

It not only offered a great chance for a new manager to make a killing, but to get well-killed on the side.

All in all, it was the toughest, biggest, deadliest and the most thrilling ranch job in America—if a man had nerve enough to take it.

Burt Mossman had plenty of nerve—so he took it. He signed the contract in late December, 1897.

He knew just what he was facing, and how slim were his chances.

··≈[*Part Three*]≈··

Hash Knife Superintendent

IT WAS around four o'clock in the morning of January 20, 1898, when Burt climbed down from the Atlantic & Pacific train at Holbrook. It was still dark, and on up front toward the engine he could see a man with a lantern scrutinizing the half-dozen arrivals.

"Reckon he didn't come," Burt heard him say to a young man in heavy work clothes.

Burt approached the pair and identified himself. The depot agent said he was the man they were looking for, but they didn't think he'd be wearing city clothes and a derby hat. Burt had wired the ranch headquarters near Joseph City, eleven miles west, that he'd arrive on this train and for a Hash Knife man to meet him. The young cowboy had come down, leading a spare horse. The through trains did not stop at Joe City, so Burt had to continue on here to the county seat.

He asked the boy if there was any place where they could get a cup of coffee and a bite to eat. The cowboy led him to the Chinaman's, down the street from the Bucket of Blood saloon.

"We ain't had a killin' in there since last summer," the boy bragged. "One more'd make it seventeen. Most of 'em been Hash Knife boys or old hands who used to work for the outfit."

The Chinaman's joint was greasy and fly-specked, and the nighthawks were mostly drunk. Burt and the boy sat at the far end of the counter and conversed in low tones. Burt allowed they might as well leave for the ranch as soon as they finished their ham and eggs. In answer to a question, the boy said his name was Charlie Fought.

When they were on their second cup of coffee, and the drunks were gone, Burt asked him how things were at the ranch. Charlie answered that Bob Morris, the ramrod and manager since Frank Jones had left, had a gang of men rounding up a trainload of big mixed-stuff over near Winslow, thirty-three miles on west. Then he added:

"We got a tip yesterday afternoon that some of them Jack-Mormons down near Snowflake had a little batch of Hash Knife steers penned up."

Burt looked up sharply. "Did you report it to the sheriff?"

"Not yet. Thought maybe we better wait until you come."

"How far is it from here?"

"About thirty miles. It's gettin' down in the rough country."

Burt turned the matter over in his mind. Maybe he had better not start on this initial visit to the ranch until he'd had a talk with the new sheriff. He knew Frank Wattron by reputation. People called him "Judge," and for several years he'd combined his drugstore business with his job as Justice of the Peace. He was a tall, witty fellow, with long, scraggly mustaches, and he placed a great deal of reliance on a sawed-off, double-barreled shotgun that he kept handy under the prescription counter.

In the November elections, just past, he had defeated Jones, the Hash Knife manager, by exactly seven votes. The story was that a renegade Mormon named Bill Smith, who was a sort of head man of the rustlers, had slapped Jones in the face with his hat, and the ranch manager had refused to accept the challenge. It cost Jones the election.

Burt asked for a third cup of coffee. He wished he knew more about the lay of the land. It might be a wise idea for him to get the sheriff to lend him a couple of deputies and ride straight on down to Snowflake, where the thieving was reported.

He was certain that this eternal stealing was his Number One problem. If he was going to succeed at the Hash Knife he'd have to break up the rustler gangs, haul them to the county jail, and then see that they were convicted. G. L. Brooks had told him in Albuquerque that in the fourteen years the Hash Knife had been operating in Arizona, they had never got a single conviction. The sheriff and his deputies would bring in thieves and have airtight cases against them. But they'd manage to slip a few friends on the jury, and the worst that had ever happened to them was a hung jury and a retrial.

Burt knew that something deep down happened to any outfit that was being stolen deaf, dumb and blind. The ranch manager and his ramrod set the pattern of efficiency and loyalty. And if they couldn't stop rustling, the spread slowly went to pieces.

Cowboys were strange individuals. When they had real leaders there was nothing they wouldn't do for their outfit, even at the risk of death. But when things were slack and discipline was gone, they lost their interest. Some of them were bound to help the thieves and even do a little rustling themselves, and before long a ranch just plumb went to hell.

Maybe right this minute was the time to strike. Why bother with the sheriff? Burt had a long-shot chance to make a big lick and set these rustlers back on their haunches. It would really mean something if he did it alone, with only this kid cowboy to pilot him.

"How long would it take us to get over to that country where they're holding our stuff?" he asked.

"Reckon 'bout five-six hours in this kind of weather. Maybe little less."

Burt asked him what he thought the thieves were going to do with the steers.

"Butcher 'em and haul 'em to a meat market when it gets dark," he answered. "Most of them Jaspers got little batches of cattle of their own, so it's easy for 'em to claim they're selling their own beef."

Burt looked the twenty-year-old boy straight in the eye. "You game to ride out there with me? Just you and me?"

"Sure. I'll go along."

"We might not come back, Charlie."

"Reckon they wouldn't get both of us."

Burt explained the odds that were against them; they would be in enemy country, and against desperate men who would have all the advantages. "Still want to try it?" he questioned.

"Say, what do you take me for?"

Burt grinned and patted his shoulder. "All right. Get the horses, and bring them to the depot." Burt had his own saddle and bridle in a sack, and he'd change to some rough clothes.

"Shall I borrow a Winchester?" Charlie asked. "I got a six-shooter."

Burt explained that they'd have a better chance not to show their weapons. They'd have to trust a good deal to luck.

Burt was standing by the door of the frame depot when Charlie came up with the horses. It was around ten above zero and he decided to wear his long, heavy dude overcoat. He slipped his .45 Colt into the right-hand side pocket.

Light was just beginning to show when they swung up in their saddles and started off.

Most of the time the two riders jogged along in silence, each man nursing his own thoughts.

Burt straightened up in his saddle and shivered a little—and it was not entirely from the cold. Maybe he was plunging in over his head. But it was too late now to turn back.

The country was getting rougher, with the trail skirting heavy clumps of cedar and dipping in and out of deep draws. Burt at least was satisfied that he had a reliable boy with him. He knew the district and apparently he had been tipped off as to the spot where the thieves had their holding pen. The riders kept to little-known trails so that there would be no suspicion of what they were doing.

When they were two or three miles from their goal, Charlie asked Mossman what he wanted him to do.

"Just watch me, Charlie, and follow suit," Burt answered.

The trail twisted around a ridge, and suddenly the two men saw a blazing campfire, and a wagon and team on ahead a hundred yards or so. There were three men nearby and when they caught sight of the approaching riders each man stepped to the wagon and picked up his rifle. The trio were on the far side of the fire, their guns loosely held in their hands.

Burt pulled up his horse sideways to the fire and swung down from his saddle. His pony was between him and the fire, with the three men on the opposite side. Behind the screen of his horse he quickly slipped his pistol from the right-hand pocket of his overcoat and shoved it up his left sleeve. Pushing his fingers into his sleeves, Chinese coolie fashion, he walked around the head of his horse and stepped to the fire.

"By God! Ain't it cold!" he said, pushing his hands deeper into his sleeves.

The three men eyed the visitors and made no answer.

"Thought we'd freeze to death," Burt went on, edging over toward the nearest of the trio.

Suddenly he jerked out his right hand and shoved his Colt into the belly of the man on his left.

"Drop your guns!" he shouted. "Drop 'em!"

The rifles clattered to the ground.

"Reach up!" Burt ordered. "Push 'em up!"

The boy had his own Colt cocked and pointed at the man on the right.

"Get the rifles, Charlie."

When the boy had stepped behind them and picked up the rifles, Burt told him to search the men for pistols. Charlie gingerly felt their hips and pockets.

He found no more arms. He and Burt now had the three unarmed men covered with their six-shooters.

Without shifting his eyes from the trio, Burt reached down for one of the rifles. He half-lowered the lever to make certain there was a shell in the chamber. Then he handed the rifle to the boy and told him to put up his own pistol.

"Stand over here, Charlie," he ordered. "If one of these bastards makes a move, kill him!"

Burt walked to the wagon and threw back the tarp. He counted the quarters of three steers. The hides were lying under a tree where the men had rigged a pulley to yank up the beef. Each hide had a big Hash Knife brand. The thieves had put off disposing of the tell-tale hides until too late.

Burt picked up a second rifle and examined the chamber. Then he pumped the shells out of the third rifle, and tossed it in the back of the beef wagon. With the rifle barrel of the loaded gun he motioned for one of the thieves to pack the hides to the wagon.

"We're driving back to Holbrook," he explained tersely. "You're all three going to ride in the wagon, and one of you'll drive the team. I'm not going to bother to tie you up. I think you're a bunch of yellow skunks. But understand—I'll kill the first man that makes a false move. Now get in there and start going."

It was thirty long, cold miles back to Holbrook. Darkness had dropped down by the time they pulled up at the side door of the courthouse. Burt sent Charlie in to locate Frank Wattron.

The sheriff knew all about Mossman and his new job, and the reputation he had made in the Bloody Basin. He warmly shook hands and congratulated him.

When the three renegade Mormons were safely behind the bars, with the branded hides tucked away in the basement of the courthouse and the beef quarters delivered to a butcher-shop, Wattron took Burt out to supper.

"How far you ready to go with this, Mossman?" he questioned.

"As far as you are, Sheriff, and then a little farther."

"That suits me down to a T," Wattron said. "I'm going to give you a deputy-sheriff's badge, and I'll assign you the best man I've got any time you want him. Between us we'll stop this damn thievin'."

-- 2 --

After supper that night, Burt told Charlie to get some sleep and they'd ride out to the ranch headquarters early the next morning. Then he drifted over to the depot to arrange to have his gear sent on out to Joe City on the morning accommodation train. He was talking to the night agent when a train of empty stock cars going west rolled by.

"That's the train for them Hash Knife cattle at Winslow," the agent announced casually. "Reckon they'll be loadin' tomorrow or the day after."

Suddenly Burt figured it might be a good idea to get over there and see first-hand how ranch matters were going on. It would give him a good chance to find what sort of cattle they were shipping out, and get a look at Bob Morris, the foreman, in action.

From what he'd been able to get out of young Charlie, he was convinced that two-thirds of the men weren't earning their salt. He sure wished he had someone he could trust, like Charlie Wall or poor Hayden Justice. Apparently Bob Morris was honest enough, but he was too easy-going. The men imposed on him. He just wasn't tough enough.

The thing to do, he concluded, was to move fast right here at the start, and find out things for himself. Last place they'd expect him would be over at the shipping pens or meeting the herd a few miles out.

He caught a train at seven o'clock that morning. It was after nine when he reached Winslow, and he went straight to the Creswell Livery Stable and asked for a good saddle horse. He explained who he was, and made discreet inquiries about the direction the trail-herd would be moving in from.

The loafers in the hot little office raised their eyebrows when they realized the identity of the newcomer. He didn't look like so very much, at that. He was a little under five feet eight and weighed 165 pounds, and his heavy rough clothes gave him the appearance of being a rather squat, thick-chested individual, with small hands and feet. That wasn't the way fighting men came in Arizona.

So this was the hombre who was going to run the Hash Knife? A burly six-footer, with thick lips and flabby face, snickered as he whispered his insult.

"What do you think of him, Montie?" a second loafer sneered.

Montgomery doubled over in laughter. The idea of this little fellow trying to run the great Hash Knife was a sure enough joke.

Burt could feel the color mounting in his face. His hands went to the buttons of his heavy coat. He'd slip it off and take to this blubbering lout.

But he turned on his heels and walked out of the room. He had other fish to fry. He'd square this up in its proper time.

Suddenly it came to him that he'd gone a long way in learning to control his temper. Five years ago, or even less than that, he'd have knocked the idiot down, and then tried his best to pick a fight with the others. But he was growing up. He'd learned a lot about self-control.

He met the foreman a few miles out of town, riding point on the herd. When they'd penned the five hundred head, he jogged alone back to the livery stable.

The gang of loafers was still there, including the noisy Montie Montgomery who had made the slurring remarks that morning. There were sly whispers and sneering grins when he entered the office.

Burt slowly took off his heavy coat and hat. Then without saying a word he walked up to the two-hundred-pound Montgomery and grabbed him by the nose. He gave it a vicious twist, and it was as effective as if he'd put a twitch on a bronc's lip.

The big loafer yelled in pain. The suddenness of the attack had caught him off guard. He rubbed his sorry beak and swore softly, but he made no move.

"If you're so damned easily amused, why don't you laugh at that?" Burt chided. His gray eyes were blazing.

The big fellow had nothing to say, and the loafers drifted off. They wanted no part of this new manager.

Burt had won Round Two. The grapevine quickly carried the word over the county that the new Hash Knife boss was no one to fool with. He and a lone cowboy had brought in three Jack-Mormons and a load of beef on his first day. And on the next he'd made a monkey out of big Montie Montgomery. Better not fool with him.

Burt soon discovered that one of the cowboys he had inherited was an old friend from his Rio Grande days. Frank Wallace had worked as wagon boss over in the Engle Ferry country the first year or so Burt was at the Monticello ranch. For several years he had been manager of the Waters Cattle Company here in Arizona, and when it had been bought by the Hash Knife outfit Frank had been sold down the river along with the cows and eighteen hundred head of horses.

Frank was a quiet-spoken, honest fellow, in his late thirties, and it had been a terrible blow to step down from manager to plain cowboy. His wife and three children lived on the borderline of poverty on Frank's forty dollars a month.

Burt asked Frank to ride the ranges with him, and in a week they covered most of the Hash Knife country. Frank didn't want to knock the outfit or his companions, but he had to give honest answers to Burt's questions.

It was obvious that the first thing to do was to clean out the old management, and then get rid of all the hands who were under the least suspicion. There were eighty-four men on the payroll, and a number of them were small ranchers and local toughs who somehow or other had figured out how to draw down pay twelve months a year, and steal a little on the side. Frank had a line on most of them.

On pay day, February 1st, exactly ten days after he arrived, Burt let Bob Morris and fifty-two men go. He appointed Frank Wallace foreman at $75 a month, and arranged for his wife to keep house for him at headquarters. This left him a winter crew of thirty-two men.

In place of six to eight men hanging around the eight linecamps, Burt kept two men in each lonely outpost. In isolated winter camps it was never safe to let one man live alone: there were too many accidents and unpredictable hazards that could happen to a lone cowboy.

That winter there was endless gossip and a hundred dire threats against the new manager. Every renegade Mormon, little-rancher cowthief, Mexican rustler and bad man in Navajo County was lined up solidly against him.

But Frank Wattron and the sheriff's office were on his side up to the hilt. Burt was sure, as well, of the county prosecuting attorney, and of the merchants and more substantial citizens all over the district. Navajo County had acquired a hard reputation that was really hurting its growth and development.

He saw, too, that he made friends with the Mormon bishop at Joe City, and with the bishop down in Snowflake, bordering the Apache country. These good men, and the majority of their faith, were definitely on the side of law and order. When the Mormons had made their early settlements in Arizona they had had a hard time with the Indians and Mexicans, and with many of the Gentiles, too, and it had turned some of the less ardent members of the flock into bitter fighting-men. It was only a step for them to forsake their religion entirely and take the offensive.

Hard citizens had emerged, as well, from the long-drawn-out feud between the Mexicans and the Americans. Over in St. Johns there had been an open race war, and the bitter hate that the Mexicans and Texans held for one another was fanned into a blazing fire.

The thousands of Hash Knife cattle, grazing on the edges of the vast holdings, offered too much of a temptation to the borderland men of this last frontier. Life was hard and dangerous, and it seemed no real crime to them to brand a few calves and steal beef to eat or sell from this rich "foreign" company that was using more than a million acres of government land without paying a penny for it. Yet, they argued, if one of their own hungry Mexicans or Mormons, or any poor settler dared run his little batch of cattle or sheep on Hash Knife range, which was actually half U. S. land, there was hell to pay.

For several years past a number of the small ranchers had drifted onto the Hash Knife payroll, and often ranch hands took up a homestead of their own. It was against orders for them to have their own brand, but ranch discipline was slack. It was easy to steal, and even if a Mexican or Jack-Mormon was caught he knew how to pack a jury with three or four of his own kind.

Burt had got rid of most of the Hash Knife cowboys who were suspect, and it wasn't long until he knew where the major part of the stealing was going on. He and Frank Wattron quickly became trusted friends, and Frank tried to impress him with the danger he was running in riding alone over the country, or even traveling with a single unarmed cowboy.

"I'll assign Joe Bargeman to go with you, Burt, if you'll take him," Frank suggested one afternoon when the two were loafing in his office. "He's the best deputy I've got."

"Well, maybe I will borrow him," Burt agreed. "I've got a hunch some of those Mexicans up around Water Canyon are helping themselves to Hash Knife stuff."

"That's where that Baca gang operate. They're tough hombres. You better take Joe with you if you go there."

But the sheriff still had to do quite a little selling job on Joe. Three or four years before this, several Hash Knife cowboys had swapped lead with a hunting party of Apaches, but it had been at long distance and nobody had been hurt. Joe rode out alone from the sheriff's office to have a look.

A sudden shot shattered the bone in Joe's right leg and a second slug killed his horse. Joe rolled into heavy brush, but his quick eye noted the spot where the bullets had come from.

All that boiling hot afternoon he lay and fought his pain. He knew if he lost consciousness he'd be signing his own death warrant. With grim courage he forced himself to concentrate on a plot of hackberry bushes down and across the trail. Finally he caught a bit of moving color. He was sure it was the red headband of an Apache.

He had to move his wounded leg to draw a bead, and he winced from the nauseating pain. When the bit of red showed in his twin sights, he squeezed the trigger. There was not even a yell, but he knew he had not missed.

He waited for long minutes, then he dragged himself across the trail and into the hackberries. He had blown off the top of the Indian's head.

Joe knew he had to get to help or he would die from loss of blood. It took him an hour to fix himself a pair of crude crutches. Half that night he crawled and hobbled down the trail to Campbell's sheep ranch. He saved his own life, but he still walked with a bad limp in his left leg.

"He's as game as a Mexican fighting cock," the sheriff concluded. "And he's just about the fastest man with a six-shooter that I ever saw. Better take him."

Burt finally agreed, and two mornings later they rode south at dawn. "Hell of a way to spend St. Patrick's Day, ain't it," Burt observed.

It was late afternoon when they pulled up in front of two cabins, set a few rods apart, at a point where the bottom of a wooded canyon widened out. Five or six men were loitering around the first cabin.

Burt and the deputy dismounted, their saddle guns in their hands. One of the Mexicans gruffly demanded what they wanted. Burt answered that they were from the sheriff's office and wanted to search the houses for stolen beef. The leader shrugged his shoulders and told them to go ahead. They motioned for him to lead the way.

They found nothing suspicious in the first cabin, but when they came out they noticed that all but the one man who had gone inside with them had drifted off into the cedars.

"We'll take a look at the other house," Burt said in Spanish.

"You got search warrant?" the Mexican demanded. He seemed to know his law terminology.

Burt was sure he couldn't read English, so he pulled out the nearest thing he had to official-looking paper and shoved it under the man's nose. Then he pocketed the paper and told Joe to lead the way. The door of the cabin was locked but the deputy managed to locate an axe and break through.

"Here's your beef!" Joe shouted.

Burt stepped inside, and sure enough the four quarters lay on the floor on top of the hide. When the two men walked outside they could see their lone Mexican loping off through the trees.

Burt sprang on his horse and raced after him, his Winchester in his right hand. He could make out a boy hurrying toward the man with a rifle. He shouted for the fugitive to stop, and when he refused Burt sabered him with his gun.

Burt dismounted and helped the man to his feet. A hundred yards on up the canyon he could see one of the Mexicans grab the rifle from the boy's hands and bring it to his shoulder. The shot kicked up the dust at Burt's feet.

Suddenly he spotted a second man on his left aiming at him. The slug ricocheted off a boulder, and a splinter from the bullet clipped a piece of flesh off the bridge of his nose. He bled as if he had been slashed with a knife.

Three men were shooting at him when he jammed his rifle into the leader's guts and told him to catch a loose saddled horse that was a few yards off. Burt still held his own mount by the reins. Forcing the Mexican to bring up his horse, he crouched down between the two animals and ordered his prisoner to point toward the cabins. That moment a rifle sounded off to his left, and Burt knew that Joe was opening up.

Suddenly the Mexican whom Burt had in tow jerked back his horse and Burt was exposed. One bullet tore off the pommel of his saddle, and a second cut one of his bridle reins squarely in two. He yelled to the Mexican to order his friends to stop their shooting or he'd kill him. It brought a lull in the firing.

It was almost dark by the time they got their prisoner back to the first cabin. Burt pushed him on ahead, with his rifle shoved into his back.

He was the toughest man he had ever had to handle. He refused to move farther until they put a noose around his head and threatened to string him up. After he had admitted that his name was Baca, they tied both his hands and legs and laid him just inside the door. They took pains to barricade it, and later made sure that if the Mexicans shot into it they'd hit their leader.

It had required a good deal of patience and skill to get their own horses into the cabin. They were sixty miles from safety and they faced a long and uncertain night of danger. Sooner or later they'd need their horses.

There were no windows in the cabin and the only door was blocked, but they could hear the men squabbling in the adjoining hut. Suddenly it occurred to both Burt and Joe that their relative positions had been reversed; they themselves were now on the defensive. They were the ones who would have to fight their way out when morning came. Their only hope lay in their hostage.

It was just breaking dawn when Burt took the ropes off the Mexican's legs and pulled him to his feet. He still had the noose around his neck. Burt cautioned him that if he made the slightest noise he'd blow out his brains.

They quietly slipped outdoors, and with the Mexican in the lead stepped close to the door of the adjoining cabin. The prisoner had his instructions.

Burt punched him with his rifle and whispered for him to go ahead. The frightened man made his speech. His captors would kill him if his compadres did not throw down their guns and come out, one at a time, with their hands in the air.

Burt jabbed him sharply and he repeated his pleading. He would be killed if they did not obey at once.

Burt now called out his own warning in Spanish. He'd count ten and if the men didn't come out before he'd finished, this Baca would be a dead hombre. Then he'd kill the rest of them.

The three men could hear oaths and violent words drift out from the cabin. Slowly Burt began his counting. When he got to seven, a voice shouted: *"Un momento, Señor!"*

Slowly the door opened and one by one they marched out into the cold light of the dawn. Joe felt over each man for a pistol. They lined up the four men, with their leader making the fifth, along the cabin, their faces to the wall. Burt stood guard with his rifle. He repeated that he'd kill the first man who made a false move.

Joe tied each man's hands behind his back. Then he picked out the youngest of the crew and, holding his gun on him, had him take five bridles and bring in the hobbled horses. Next he ordered him to put on the saddles and help the men to mount. He securely tied the feet of each of the prisoners under his horse.

It was two minutes' work to fasten each bridle rein to the tail of the horse ahead. Full daylight had come by the time the little procession took up the hard grind to Holbrook.

Both Burt and Joe knew they were taking a long chance with the law. During the night the Mexicans in the cabin had cut up the hide and disposed of it. Consequently they were bringing in five men with no real evidence against them.

But they figured that men wouldn't fight this hard, and be as tough as they had been, unless they were deadly afraid of some sort of consequences.

"I'll bet they've been stealing horses," Burt suggested to the sheriff, when they'd delivered their prisoners, worn and hungry, and utterly exhausted.

"We'll hold 'em incommunicado for a spell, and see if we can get 'em to talk," Wattron proposed.

Two weeks went by, and despite pressure and a promise of

leniency to any of them who would turn state's evidence, they could get nothing. Their women had followed them into Holbrook, and finally Wattron gave way enough to permit the women to send in fresh clothes and get the filthy garments of the prisoners to wash.

Burt happened to be in the courthouse when the dirty linen was gathered, and he asked Wattron to let him search through the bundle. It was a vile, smelly job, but it paid off. Sure enough, in the armpit of one shirt he found three crudely scribbled words: "*Mueve los caballos.*"

"Look at this, Frank!" Burt showed him his discovery. " 'Move the horses'! They're horse thieves, sure as you're a foot high."

Burt and Joe Bargeman and two more deputies combed the Water Canyon country and found sixteen big work horses that had been stolen from the alfalfa farmers along the Salt River. By a promise of court immunity to one man they built up an airtight case: this Baca gang had long shuttled horses stolen in lower Arizona on up into Utah, and they brought stolen Utah horses on south toward the Mexican border.

But catching a thief was only half the story, here in the Territory of Arizona. He still had to be convicted and sentenced in open court.

It would be some months before the fall term opened in Holbrook. And unless Burt, with the sheriff's help, could make some powerful medicine, the juries were almost certain to be hung and all the work would be for nothing.

He could capture all the rustlers in northern Arizona, but if he couldn't get them convicted the whole thing would backfire in his face.

-- 3 --

Burt had a lot to do that spring besides fighting rustlers. The stock had come through the winter in good shape and there was every prospect of a big calf crop. On the first of June his two wagons started combing a country roughly fifty by a hundred miles square.

With the single exception of the XIT ranch in west Texas, it was probably the largest cattle operation in the United States. The only other spread that surpassed it on the continent was the great Terrazas property that sprawled over a vast country in Chihuahua, and ran better than a quarter-million head of cattle and thousands of horses and mules.

But Burt was so sure that his ultimate success depended on stopping thieving that he left most of the details of the round-up and branding to Frank Wallace and a lean, quiet Texan named Pete Pemberton. Pete had been imported during the days of the sheep wars, and was one of the few gun-fighters who knew when to quit. Burt made him wagon boss, and assigned him to the outfit that gathered to the west between Winslow and Flagstaff.

This Hash Knife was a curious outfit. The brand had been established in the late '70's by three men from Waterford, Texas, and a big herd collected on the Middle Fork of the Brazos.

Early in 1880 the cattle were turned loose in a vast stretch of land that ran south along the Pecos from Seven Rivers, New Mexico, and then east two hundred miles to the Fort Stockton country. It was joined on the north by John Chisum's mighty Jinglebob outfit.

In 1885, toward the end of the great cattle boom, the flow of Texas cattle stock was being checked by northern quarantine regulations, and the outfit decided to move out from the Pecos. Thirty thousand steers had been sent to the Little Missouri country in Montana. And shortly after the Atlantic & Pacific—later to be called the Santa Fé—pushed across northern Arizona, 30,000 head of Hash Knife cows and yearlings were unloaded at Holbrook and Winslow in Arizona. The Aztec Land & Cattle Company, by buying from the railroad a million acres of government-donated railroad land, had free use of every alternate section. In a bit of international finance, $500,000 worth of bonds were sold to German investors, and when dividends failed to appear, Seligman Bros. of New York bought in the bonds at half-price, and with them went virtual control of the ranching company. Certain officials and directors of the railroad were tied into the outfit and its management.

The southern portion of the range was largely rough, timbered country, but the outfit more than equalized matters by running at least five thousand head on the free grass north of the tracks, bordering the vast Navajo Reservation.

From the start hard luck seemed to pursue both the Montana and the Arizona ventures of the great Hash Knife. The terrible winter of 1886–7 had practically wiped out the 30,000 steers that had been trailed into Montana. When spring broke, Simpson himself hurried to Montana and sent out six wagons to round up what was left of his herds. They combed the country as far south as Nebraska, but they gathered a scant 600 out of the 30,000.

The puzzle of why they found no great number of dead Hash Knife cattle was not solved until Simpson figured that the herds had drifted into draws and deep coulees with the storms, and there frozen or starved to death; when the great spring thaws came and the chinooks melted the deep snow, the floods had washed thousands of head down the creeks into the Missouri.

The awful blizzards of that winter had not swept down as far as Arizona, and the southern Aztec ranges had escaped the tragedy. But in these early years they had faced drouths and low prices and the great sheep invasions that had brought on the Tonto Basin war. Texas gun-fighters had been imported to protect Hash Knife interests. One of them was Tom Pickett, who'd fought alongside Billy the Kid. Four or five of the hired killers died with their boots on; but by '88, when the Basin war degen-

erated from a straight cattle-sheep war to a bitter personal feud between the Graham and the Tewkesbury factions, the Hash Knife had pulled out its gun-fighters.

But the dirty work had been done and from then on the outfit suffered from general stealing. Renegade Mormons led the list of thieves, but disgruntled Hash Knifers and outlaw Mexicans all helped themselves. No dividends were ever paid on Aztec company capital stock, and no convictions secured in the whole-sale stealing.

Pete Pemberton's wagon worked in close association with the wagon of the C O Bar outfit, which the following year was taken over by the Babbitt Brothers of Winslow. Several smaller ranchers sent reps. Frank Wallace took out the eastern wagon, and among the reps who would eat his grub was a cowboy named Cameron from the Esperanza Cattle Company, managed by

Will C. Barnes, at this time head of the Territorial Sanitary Board.

Burt had been made inspector for northern Arizona, and it attested to his reputation for scrupulous honesty for him to be assigned to check over every shipment of his own cattle. Incidentally it gave him an additional income equal to his ranch pay. He was doing right good for himself and his goose was hanging high.

He had already paid a visit to the horse range over by Sunset Pass, twenty miles south of Winslow. Two men lived here in a tight stone cabin, and every day they rode a fifteen-mile circle on four hundred Hash Knife horses and in addition eighteen hundred head that had been acquired from the Waters Cattle Company.

Burt threw a jaundiced eye at the Waters stock. They looked good and they were fat and spry, but he knew most of them would hardly see twenty again. As far as he could tell, they weren't actually worth their salt.

Back at Holbrook he heard rumors of an English outfit that was buying horses for the Chinese government. He got in touch and arranged for the head buyer to look over the stuff. The Englishman explained they could use a trainload, but each animal must be carefully tested for wind.

Burt had his boys gather around 500 head and rough-break them. Then he appeared with his buyer. One by one the horses were brought out, saddled and ridden out a hundred yards at a walk and trot by his most trusted boys. At the marking post each horse would be turned and brought in at the gallop. It was an easy test, even for fat and ancient plugs that would have fallen down if the distance had been three or four miles. When it was all over Burt deposited a certified check for $10,400 for 520 horses at $20 the round. It was almost like found money, as far as the ranch was concerned.

Later on he shipped out two trainloads of Waters horses to Kansas and sold them at $6.50 a head. Eventually he disposed of the 400 remnants to two Mormon boys at Joseph City for $4 the round. They were four years running down the horses and barely got their bait back. Burt certainly had learned how to be a good trader.

A few weeks before his June round-up began Burt and his foreman took eight or ten men and once again rode west to the horse camp. This time they were concerned only with young Hash Knife stock. It took grain-fed mounts to corral these snorty broncs and the men spent a week cutting-out some two hundred of the most likely-looking four- and five-year-olds.

Burt had a first-class peeler and horse-judge in Windy Bill Bawcon. When a gelding was chosen he was roped and thrown, and rawhide hobbles put on his front feet.

The remuda and the recruits were slowly driven to head-quarters and turned into a big fenced pasture. Bill always had a bunch of broncs held here, and every couple weeks he would bring in eight head and rough them out. His job was to see that there were plenty of tough young horses for the hard work of the spring and fall round-ups. The breaking corral was close to headquarters, and besides being well-watered it was convenient to haystacks.

Burt was just back from the horse camp when word arrived that the United States had declared war on Spain. A few days later he received a letter from Buckey O'Neil over in Prescott. Buckey was an Easterner who fitted the Western frontier like a kid glove does a dandy's hand. He wallowed in danger and long chances. At the start he lost most of his money bucking the monte games and the roulette wheels, and save for a reputation for cool recklessness and generosity, about all he got out of it was his nickname of Buckey. He had served a term as sheriff of

Yarapi County and this spring of '98 he was editing a cattleman's magazine called *Hoofs and Horns*.

Buckey was authorized by Leonard Wood and Teddy Roosevelt to organize a company of mounted men in the Prescott country for the Rough Riders. Buckey was well-acquainted with Burt and he wanted him to enlist in his outfit. He was sure he could get Burt a commission.

Burt came from a fighting family that traced back to the American Revolution. He knew how it would please his father for him to join up, but he had his work cut out for him right here. If he left now the countryside would think he couldn't stand the gaff, and that the thieves and outlaws had run him off.

He pondered over the proposition for a day or two, and then wrote Buckey and explained how tied up he was with his private war against the rustlers. Three months later Buckey was cut down by a Spanish bullet on the slopes of San Juan Hill in Cuba. It was a nice sort of play war—but real enough for the gallant Buckey.

Starting in June, Burt split his time three ways: he spent one third with each of his two wagons and the remaining third quietly riding the outskirts of his ranges with deputy sheriff Joe Bargeman. Burt was sure he and Joe had put a temporary crimp in the wholesale thieving that had been going on before he came. But he was still worried about how many men he could actually convict, and send down to the hell-hole of the Territorial prison at Yuma. That would be the real test.

The round-ups and calf branding were old routine for Burt. The technique was exactly the same that he had followed for the six years he was with the Monticello outfit in New Mexico, only here in Arizona there were fewer outside reps and wagons. Consequently, it was less confusing and the problem of holding the cuts of neighboring ranches was almost nil.

During the hot June and July weeks, each of his two wagons

gathered and branded around two hundred Hash Knife calves daily. Often the various line-camps would be used; and in certain localities there were holding corrals that made the job hardly more than half as hard and exhausting as when the work was done in the open. Several times the individual wagons turned in calf-branding tallies of as many as four hundred head in a single day.

It was the largest branding the Hash Knife had had in its history. The winter had been mild, the spring grass good, and the calves were big and strong. And obviously Burt's fight against the rustlers had cut down the thieving and added to the count.

By far the safest method for stealing stock was to hide out a bunch of cows and calves, and when the calves were branded pen them up and run off the mothers. The country along the southern edge of the Hash Knife range was rough and covered with pine and cedar, and so cut by deep draws and hidden valleys, that this sort of stealing was almost impossible to stop.

But Burt and the faithful Joe Bargeman, suddenly appearing as if on a magic carpet in some far-away corner or hidden canyon, put the fear of God in scores of little thieves. The word was abroad that this pair would shoot to kill.

When the last tally of the branding was in, Burt added up the long column. The two wagons had branded 16,000 calves.

And there were eleven men in the county jail under indictment for cattle stealing.

Things were looking up around the Hash Knife.

-- 4 --

The fall term of court opened at Holbrook on a Tuesday. Colonel Wilson, the attorney for the Aztec Land & Cattle Company, arrived from Prescott the day before. Wilson was a distinguished gentleman of the old school, who had served as Territorial Delegate to the United States Congress.

During the past fourteen years he had tried his level best to get convictions of men charged with stealing Hash Knife cattle, but they had always managed to pack the jury with their friends. A number of times he had insisted on second and even third trials, but invariably the jury would fail to agree. In the end the county, short of funds, could do nothing but turn loose the obviously guilty men.

Previous to the court session Burt quietly went to the Mormon bishops at Joe City and Snowflake. He frankly told them he wanted to put this whole question of Mormon thieves squarely up to decent churchmen. He was going to have Colonel Wilson quietly ask the prosecuting attorney and the sheriff's office to pick only Mormon jurors in cases involving renegade Mormons. What happened then would be strictly up to the bishops.

It was a ticklish business, and Burt was not at all certain how much authority the honest Mormon leaders would have over the rank and file of their churchmen. But it was the one chance for conviction he had and he played it to the hilt.

When the trial of the first of the three Jack-Mormons opened Burt winked at Sheriff Wattron as one Mormon of good reputation after another was accepted by the prosecuting attorney. Within an hour the whole panel was chosen, and Burt and the cowboy were called in as witnesses.

By eleven the following morning Judge Sloan had given his instructions to the jury and the twelve men were locked in the back room. The next half-hour was a little trying for Burt and the law enforcers. Then the jury sent word to the Judge that they had reached a verdict, and they were marched back to the box.

The foreman was a lean, red-faced pioneer and when he stood up and faced the Judge there was dead silence in the courtroom.

"We find the defendant guilty," he said in a strained voice, and sat down.

Verdicts for the two remaining Jack-Mormons came quickly. Next came the cases of the five Mexicans.

This time the program was for the prosecution to see that the jurors were straight Anglos, and honorable men. The machinery of justice was now well oiled, and the convictions came in a deadly monotonous order.

The Judge waited until all the eleven cases were disposed of before he fixed the sentences. They ranged from two years to the limit of four years in the state penitentiary.

When the tedious job was finished, Burt and Judge Sloan stood together looking out of the window of his chambers at the dreary scene below. Most of the men sentenced were miserable creatures whose families were poor and would have a hard time while their men were in prison. If Burt had not hated all thieves with such bitter intensity he probably would have tried to have the Judge soften some of the sentences. But a thief was a thief to him.

They watched a woman with a gray shawl wrapped around her thin body, make her way across the wind-swept, bare courthouse yard. It was desolate and cold and melancholy.

"Who's that woman?" Judge Sloan asked, turning to Burt.

"That's the wife of that fellow King."

"Poor soul," the Judge uttered. "I just sentenced him to three years."

Burt had nothing to say, but he was troubled later when he heard that one of his cowboys was living with the woman. When her husband came back from Yuma there were two new babies in the shack.

Burt took no chances of a slip-up in justice, and rode on down to Yuma with Joe Bargeman and one other deputy to see the men safe in the miserable, inhuman prison, squatting on the banks of the Colorado, in the scorching desert of southwestern Arizona.

On the way north he stopped off at Phoenix to see old friends, and on the second morning he dropped in at the Governor's office.

"You're doing great work up there in Navajo County, Mossman," Governor Murphy congratulated him. "But you better organize or you'll get killed."

"We're already organized, Governor," Burt answered. "Mossman & Wattron is the name of our company."

The Governor grinned. Then he went on soberly: "Don't be afraid of killing those outlaws if you have to, Burt. Take no long chances trying to arrest them. If you do have to kill any of them, and you get arrested and convicted, I'll pardon you before the ink is dry on your commitment."

It was a matter of considerable satisfaction to Burt, but he knew the dangers he was running. The leader of the toughs around Holbrook was a big, hard-shelled Jack-Mormon named

Bill Young. He ran a batch of cattle on the far side of the Little Colorado, and most of his critters carried worked-over brands. He was good at it, and he was equally skilful at keeping out of jail.

One night in the Bucket of Blood saloon in Holbrook he took on a cargo of rotgut whiskey and made a long speech about how he was going to cut down Mossman the first time he saw him. Burt walked in that minute and the bartender gave him the wink and nodded his head toward the outside door. But Burt wasn't doing any run-out.

He heard Young sounding-off in the back end of the long room. Burt's .45 Colt was tucked under the waistband of his trousers, barely covered by the edges of his coat. He figured that this was as good a time as any to see how game this big bully really was. If there had to be a showdown he might as well let it be now.

Bill Young saw him coming and his right hand fell to the butt of his pistol, stuck in his holster. But a man sitting in an arm-chair at a table is under severe handicap against a man on his feet with his hands free and easy.

"Bill, you better get your hand off that gun," Burt said quietly, looking down at him. Mossman was calm and there was a dis-arming grin on his lips. But his gray eyes were as cold as chilled steel.

"You know you ain't really tough, Bill. You just think you're tough." He stood squarely over the drunk and eyed him. "Any time you want me to, I'll prove it to you."

Young slumped forward in his chair and his two hands were now on the table. Burt slowly turned and walked the length of the saloon. Out in the street he hitched up his trousers and walked over toward Wattron's drugstore. He'd heard there was a nice little poker game going on upstairs.

He felt pretty lucky, so he figured he'd give it a whirl.

-- 5 --

That fall Burt gathered and shipped out enough beef to make up ten trainloads. That meant somewhere between four and five thousand head. It would pay expenses for the year.

He also filled an order from J. V. Vickers, a beef subcontractor at the San Carlos Indian Reservation, for four hundred head of

big steers. Burt had them cut out from the stuff gathered around Mormon Lake, and trailed the ninety miles on east to Holbrook.

The contract called for the steers to be delivered to Ash Creek, a good hundred miles to the south, in the heart of the roughest and most inaccessible mountains of Arizona. Burt chose Barney Styles, one of his top riders, to do the trail driving. Styles asked for three cowboys, and a cook and a wrangler with a small remuda and six packmules. He could take in five times the number of cattle just as easy as he could this little batch.

Burt rode out the first day or two with the herd, to be sure everything moved along nicely. A couple weeks later Barney reported back.

He had led his big steers down off the eastern end of Mogollon Rim, across the White River and the Black River, in and out of great canyons and deep draws, along mountainsides and over

rocky trails that wound through heavy timber. He had gone days and nights without water, but he'd got there. He'd lost only four head, and the big steers were in such good shape when he counted them out for Vickers, that he gladly paid the $24 a round.

This was company business, but Burt already had tried his hand at Indian contracts on his own hook. A year or two before in Phoenix, while he was still at the Bloody Basin, he'd met W. E. Travis of Salt Lake. Travis was a business man with some little political backing, who was anxious to make a killing on Indian contracts. He also had his sights set for a quick fortune from Star Route mail contracts. He figured the two sort of went together.

He needed an experienced, practical man in the field for both of his ventures, and when he met Mossman he knew he'd found his man. Burt had considerable spare time hanging on his hands during off seasons, and he wasn't adverse to turning a dollar. The first job he did in his partnership was to pick up a herd of two-year-old steers in Sonora and turn them over to J. E. Boggs, on a subcontract for the San Carlos Apaches. They didn't do too badly on that one.

The next contract Travis annexed was to supply 1,500,000 pounds of beef for the Blackfoot Reservation in northwestern Montana. Burt was dubious about it, and he finally located a man who had got together a big bunch of heavy, aged Mexican oxen, and he slipped him the contract when he wasn't looking. Burt knew they would lose plenty of money on that one.

He was at the Hash Knife when Travis got the contract for 1,750,000 pounds of beef for the San Carlos Reservation. That would mean roughly 1,750 head of big steers. In his anxiety to land the business, Travis had talked himself into making too low a bid. Burt searched for a loophole that would let them out with their eyeteeth intact.

In looking into the contract he discovered that it carried with it certain valuable grazing rights on the reservation. The old cattleman who had lost this latest contract had been delivering beef to the agency and had been running his own herds on the reservation. If he was put off the grass he'd simply have to sell out at a loss.

Burt promptly sent word to the cowman that he'd have to move off his stock, as Mossman & Travis wanted to put their own cattle on the range. Facing ruin, the rancher appealed to Burt as a fellow-cattleman. Couldn't he make some arrangement so that he could keep his cattle on the reservation?

Burt assured him his last wish was to make it tough for him. He'd like to help him. But if he and Travis kept their beef contract, he'd simply have to insist they have the range.

Finally Burt made his proposition. As a special favor to an old brother-cowman, they would let him take over their contract. He jumped at the chance, and Burt always figured that he and his partner saved themselves several thousand dollars by their generosity.

All in all, Mossman & Travis never made a penny on their beef contracts. The same thing was also largely true when it came to their Star Route mail contracts. The law was explicit that the contractor could not subcontract his routes, but it was universally broken.

After Burt had taken over the Hash Knife, he and his partner put in a bid to run a mail and passenger stage route three times a week from Holbrook southwest a hundred and ten miles to Young, via Heber. When they received the formal approval, they immediately sublet the contract to Sheriff Frank Wattron.

Things went along smoothly until a post-office inspector came out from Washington. He put a bottle of whiskey in the pocket of his coat, and climbed up alongside of the driver to make the ride to Young. He oiled the rusty tongue of the local man, and before the bottle was half empty he was hearing how the stage was being actually run by Wattron and not by Mossman.

Burt promptly lost the contract, but when new bids were opened he got it back, and at a thousand dollars more a year. But there wasn't any real money in it. And the same was true with a contract to carry the mail from Tombstone, down near the Mexican border, back and forth fourteen times a week to Fairbanks.

But it all added to the sum total of Burt's education. He was learning the different ways that different things were done, and he was learning them the hard way. He took good care to make sure that he never let his private business interfere with his company duties and loyalties.

In and out of season he plugged away on his war against thieving. Mostly he was concerned with cattle rustlers, but now and again he would go after horse thieves. The first fall he was at the Hash Knife he got a tip that there were some suspicious horses carrying the Hash Knife brand over east in the country between Springer and Tucumcari, in northern New Mexico. Burt decided he'd handle the project himself.

Empty-handed and mad enough at his failure to bite a tenpenny nail in two, Burt rode into the little cowtown of Springer late one Saturday night. The saloon occupied the front of the hotel, and Burt registered at the lower end of the bar. He was assigned a room, and told to go on back in the kitchen and maybe the girl there would get him something to eat.

Burt talked the pert young waitress into laying him out some supper on the kitchen table, and then he dragged his tired body up the stairs to his room, directly over the bar. The sound of strident, drunken voices floated up through the thin floor, but Burt figured it would take a lot more than plain noise to keep him awake.

He had just pulled off his boots and pants when a bullet tore up through the floor, a foot or two away from his chair. He heard ribald laughter and shouts, and he thought he could distinguish the word "tenderfoot." Well, he'd show them how a tenderfoot did things.

Pulling the mattress from the bed, he rolled it up and dragged it to a corner. He was just reaching for his rifle when a second slug ripped up from the bar. He perched himself on top of his rolled mattress, and leaning over the side of his barricade, emptied his 30-40 Winchester into the floor. He learned later that one bullet knocked a glass out of a customer's hand, and another slug cut a neat hole in a hat brim.

There was a sudden exodus. The entrance door was jammed in a moment, and brave men took to the windows. Burt, with his anger suddenly turned to mirth, saw one large patron hitting it down the moonlit road with a window frame draped over his shoulders.

Years later Burt spent a rollicking evening in New York with the distinguished writer of Western tales, the late Alfred Henry Lewis. They took turns spinning their yarns and Lewis finally told of the time a harmless-looking tenderfoot, who was probably Billy the Kid, had turned the tables on a drunken mob in Springer, New Mexico, and how his bullets whistling down through the ceiling had cleaned out a tough bar. He added that he had led the retreat through a side window, taking out the window sash as he dived into the street.

Burt exploded. When he could talk again, he explained that he was the villain who had cut loose with his 30-40 Winchester.

It was as good an excuse as any for the two master story-spinners to make a night of it.

The rifle that Burt had used that night in Springer was one of three that he had ordered from St. Louis. Back in the Bloody Basin days he had handled a new, high-powered rifle that belonged to a scion of the McCormick family of Chicago, and he had fallen in love with it.

Once he was dug in at the Hash Knife, he ordered three of the new 30-40 Winchesters, and presented one to Sheriff Frank Wattron and one to Joe Bargeman. Frank wanted to try out the gun immediately, when Burt told him how he had sent a bullet through a cottonwood that measured one hundred and three inches in circumference.

Burt had been working up a deer and wild turkey hunt, and he asked Wattron to go along. There were six men in the party: Mossman, Wattron, Joe Pratt, who ran a book and stationery store in Phoenix, Peg Leg Jud Lathrop, who had lost a limb in a battle with rustlers, Tom Hesser, owner of the Winslow Hotel, and a cook. Two of them, Joe Pratt and Peg Leg, took their hunting seriously. They wanted game; they weren't after sport.

A quarter-mile from their camp on Wildcat Canyon, Burt and Wattron noted the tracks of wild turkeys under a bunch of very tall pines. On the left, the wall of the canyon gradually rose to a mesa about a hundred and fifty feet above them. Wattron figured out that the turkeys roosted all night in the limbs of the tall trees, flew down in the early morning, drank in the creek and then fed as they walked up the slope. That afternoon toward twilight the two men sat with their backs to the bottom of the cliff and silently waited.

Before long the turkeys waddled up to the rim of the canyon high above, and then one by one took off, floating down to the valley as gracefully as if they were parachuting. They drank at the little stream, gobbled around, and then with a great clatter of wings flew up into the high limbs. It was too much like shooting ducks in a barrel for the two real sportsmen to kill the birds while they were on the ground. And besides it was too dark to see well.

There was a full moon that night and after supper Burt and

the sheriff went back to the trees. By exercising skill and patience they managed to maneuver around until they could get the big birds in line between them and the moon. The turkeys, high in the tree, looked no larger than robins. It took fine shooting but they managed to drop three or four birds.

Joe Pratt and Peg Leg were very excited the following morning when they saw the bag. They insisted that the two hunters show them the spot and explain how they made their kill.

Joe made no comment, but he had an idea. He came back to the camp at noon and quietly got out his shell-loading outfit and, unloading a full box of shotgun shells, reloaded them with BB shot. If he had had buckshot along he would have used that.

"No real sportsman would shoot sitting turkeys with a shot-gun," Wattron, ably assisted by Burt, challenged him.

But Joe Pratt knew what he wanted. It was game—not *the* game.

Burt quietly waited until Pratt had finished reloading his shells before he made a tour of the camp. He came back and reported that three horses were missing. All hands better help search. If Joe and Peg Leg would go on east he and Wattron would work up the canyon, while the rest of the men tried to cut sign to the west.

As soon as Joe Pratt was out of sight, the two plotters hurried back to camp. They got out his reloading outfit, took out the BB shot and packed gravel in the shells. Then they went back to their fake horse hunting. By some miracle the horses seemed to come back by themselves.

Pratt hurried through his supper, then he started down the canyon to the batch of trees. He'd get himself at least a half-dozen fat birds. Peg Leg was invited to go along as a witness.

When they were out of sight, Burt, Wattron and Tom Hesser opened a pint, broke out cigars and enjoyed themselves. Shortly they heard the first blast of Joe's shotgun.

One by one, during the next hour, they counted the shots from Pratt's trusty gun. When the count was twenty they put out their cigars, and quickly finished what was left of the bottle. Joe'd be coming back now and they would be fast asleep.

They could hear him cursing quietly as he commented to Peg Leg on his singular hard luck.

"Goddam idiots!" he swore from deep within his heart. "Damn fools! Sayin' those birds weren't more than sixty-seventy feet from the ground!"

They could hear him throw down his gun in utter disgust. "Goddam trees!" he went on. "They're three hundred feet high, if they're an inch! The damn ignorant idiots!"

No sound came from the villains. Nor did anyone tell the Phoenix hunter the truth on the following morning.

That night he joined the rifle brigade and did succeed in bringing down the champion bird of the hunt, a magnificent 24-pound gobbler.

But no one ever told about the gravel-loaded shells. You just couldn't do that to Joe Pratt; his entire faith in mankind would have been destroyed.

-- 6 --

Burt had a good many reasons to feel rather proud of his showing as the new superintendent of the great Hash Knife spread. He and Frank Wattron had become such intimates that he didn't mind talking over with the sheriff how well he'd done.

Frank had invited him to go into a pool with himself, Tom Hesser and Harry Burbage in the building of an opera house in Winslow. The town was a division point of the Santa Fé, and it was a bustling, growing community. Burt put up his quarter of the cost of the brick building, with its 880 seats.

It opened with an Italian opera, with the leading role taken by a slightly shopworn German soprano. Later Burt and Wattron were tipped off that the Santa Fé contemplated moving their shops and division point from Winslow, and they quietly sold out their holdings at a nice profit.

That late fall of '98 things couldn't have been brighter for Burt. He was thirty-one years old, in perfect health, and he enjoyed a wide reputation as the highly successful manager of one of the biggest ranches in America.

Letters from the top men of the Aztec Land & Cattle Company carried high praise for his work. In the past there had been some talk of cleaning out the cattle and liquidating the ranch, but his record branding of 16,000 calves, coupled with the fact that he'd sent a dozen of the worst rustlers over to Yuma, had led them to reject the idea of winding up the outfit.

Burt and Wattron, tramping the lonely cedar country around Cheveron Creek, had many good talks together. Frank was an older man and he pointed out to Burt that he was really only starting his career. Some day he'd count his own cattle on a thousand hills. Just don't get too gay with the rustlers and end up with a bullet through his belly.

The two weeks' hunting trip was almost over when late one afternoon angry clouds gathered in the north and a high wind started sweeping down. The following morning when the men crawled out from under their tarps there was almost a foot of snow on the ground. The Norther had struck with little warning, and it was still blowing fiercely.

They broke camp as quickly as possible, and started the pack-mules north toward Holbrook. They made it late the second afternoon, but they were exhausted and half-frozen when they turned in at the livery stable.

Burt was not worried about himself or his companions. What filled his mind was the sight of hundreds of hungry, freezing Hash Knife cows standing with their backs to the swirling snow. Cattle, with their split hooves, could not paw through the snow to the grass, like horses.

Frank consoled him with the fact that it had been six or eight years since the Little Colorado country had really faced a long, hard winter. Maybe this was only a December storm, that would blow over in another day or two. A warm Arizona sun could easily melt away the snow and let the cattle find the sun-cured grass.

The blizzard did check itself in another twenty-four hours, but the promised warm sun turned out to be only a cold, inhuman orbit that kept the high air well below freezing in the daytime. At nights the mercury dropped to near zero.   •

Not since he had lived as a boy in Minnesota had Burt experienced any such weather. He bought himself heavy underwear and a sheepskin coat, with warm overshoes and a fur cap. Almost without a break for weeks on end he and Frank Wallace rode the ranges, from one line-camp to another.

For two days they were snowbound in the rough, timbered country around Beaver Creek, while a fresh blizzard piled up more snow. Thousands of Hash Knife cows and young animals moved southward into the draws and canyons and the wooded areas. But they could find no grass. And the cold seeped into their hearts.

A hundred times Burt thought of the starving Monticello cattle, back in the days of the terrible dry-up in the early 90's. That was pitiful enough. The enemies then had been hunger and thirst from the long drouth. Here in northern Arizona new villians appeared—cold and snow that blanketed every spear of grass.

At times it seemed to Burt that it was almost a personal affront of Nature, or God, or the Invisible Force, working against him. Maybe he had been a little too proud and self-confident. But certainly he did not deserve this.

Riding back to Holbrook one clear, cold afternoon, Burt pulled up at the rim of the vast, limitless basin that spread out to the north until it lost itself in the distant horizons of Navajo land. The sun was a ball of molten steel off to the left, and the snow and ice that covered this Painted Desert, with its slender peaks and minarets and far-away mesas, suddenly seemed to burst into flame.

His horse stood motionless, as if sensing the strange mood, and Burt was conscious only of the beauty and wonder of the moment. It was as if he were a boy again, bound for the Hat ranch, as he topped the St. Augustine Pass looking down for the first time on the great Tularosa Basin. That was fifteen years ago.

He had worked and sweated and pulled this failure of a ranch up by its bootstraps. He had risked his life, time and again, to stop the theiving. In a terrific outburst of energy he had faithfully gathered every cow, and branded 16,000 calves. He was riding free and easy on the highroad to complete victory.

Then this storm with its two feet of snow buried him and his hopes. His chances of success now were as dead as one of the giant petrified trees that lay to the south in the great, weird Forest of the Long Ago.

He pulled up his bridle and spoke gently to his horse. It was dark when he reached Holbrook.

For ten straight weeks the snow covered the Hash Knife country. In his letters to his directors Burt gradually added to his earlier estimates of what the losses would be. At the start he had suggested the toll might be a thousand or two. It went up to five thousand. Finally, when the last of the snow melted, and the weak, bawling critters could get to the grass, he put the figure at ten thousand head.

Once again Burt had an overwhelming sense of failure engulf him. At least one of the two age-old enemies of all cowmen— bad weather and low prices—had played him false. He had checked the rustling and thieving, cut expenses to the bone and put the Hash Knife on its feet. But now the Elements had betrayed him.

The company officials made it clear that he was in nowise to blame, but they suggested that he had better get rid of the bulls, and at the spring round-up cut out and ship the beef and all the dry stuff.

Burt quietly nursed a hunch while he started out his two round-up wagons. When he'd got them going he took the

Santa Fé for Dodge City. In the country that stretched on west the fifty-five miles to Garden City, Kansas, he located a number of fenced range-pastures that he was able to lease.

Back at the Hash Knife he threw his cuts into age and sex groups. Most of that summer he shipped out a trainload every day, assigning them to special pastures in western Kansas. One trainload, or instance, would have only yearling steers, and would go to a certain town and pasture. The next train might be yearling heifers, or big steers, or dry cows, and each would be sent to its proper designation.

By the time the fall round-up was over and the final shipment made, Burt wrote the company that the total figure of the great exodus was 33,000 head. And there were still the calves and cows left.

But Burt wasn't finished. In Kansas City he arranged with Tom Emmen, head of the K. C. Livestock Association, to bring out the buyers. The prospective purchasers would leave Kansas City in the evening, and unload from their Pullman at Dodge City the next morning. After a breakfast at the Harvey restaurant, Burt or his representative would drive the men to the exact pasture that held the type and age of cattle wanted.

When the final check was made Burt showed an average of $14 for the 33,000 head—almost a half-million dollars in cash. It was a good 25 percent more than the owners had anticipated.

Burt was busy, but he always took time out to follow up any tips that had to do with rustling. In the late spring he and the Mormon bishop at Snowflake exchanged messages over the military telegraph, about a batch of sixty cows and calves that the bishop had seen being driven through the Mormon settlement on east into the wooded hill country.

It was late afternoon when Burt and Deputy Joe Bargeman pulled out from Holbrook. They rode all night and it was daylight when they came to the Mormon bishop's house. His two wives were getting breakfast, and Burt and Joe were invited to partake. It was a pretty slim meal, and when they finished Burt asked the bishop if he'd ever heard the story of the hog grower in Missouri. The Morman grinned and said he hadn't.

"Well," Burt began, "one day a friend from town visited the farmer. The pigs were squealing like they were starved to death, and the visitor asked him what was the matter.

" 'You see, I like my bacon streaked with strips of fat and lean,' the farmed answered. 'This happens to be the day to put on the lean.' "

The good bishop repeated the story to his wives, and they had a big laugh. They meant well enough even if they had served a lean breakfast, because when Burt and Joe rode off they had two big loaves of unleavened bran bread, and a chunk of cold meat, tied in a flour sack behind Joe's saddle. (In telling the story, Burt always added that when he next visited the bishop his wives had presented him with bouncing babies, that had arrived just five days apart.)

For a couple of hours Burt and Joe rode east along a rough wagon road. It was easy to follow the trail left by the cows and calves. When it swung off the road and pointed on up a long, deep draw, with a high mountain on the right and a rimrock and mesa on the left, the trailers took to the bench. Below in the valley they might run into trouble before they knew it.

They rode cautiously and it wasn't long until they were convinced that there was a camp a quarter-mile or so on up the canyon.

They tied up their horses and found a clump of brush on the lip of the rimrock where they could conceal themselves while they studied the narrow valley below. It was hot, and before long they started in on their single canteen of water. There was a green spot a little farther up in the basin, and they were sure there must be a spring somewhere nearby.

Joe was positive the rustlers' camp wouldn't be more than a hundred yards or so beyond this, and he was for a surprise attack on the outfit before dark. When the canteen was emptied, he pressed hard for quick action. But Burt only shook his head.

That night they rode their horses bareback down to the spring, making as little noise as possible. At daybreak they again took up their vigil, but shortly shifted farther on up the wooded top of the canyon. Suddenly they could see men below moving in and out of a heavy clump of cedars. They were pretty sure they counted five in all.

Toward noon two of them hitched up a team and drove back down the canyon. Joe begged Burt to open fire on them.

"You take the bozo drivin' and I'll cut the buttons off the other fellow," he pleaded, sighting down the barrel of his 30-40 Winchester.

Burt knew that the renegade Mormons were thick around this neck of the woods, and that they must act cautiously. He told Joe to take it easy.

The two officers slipped down to the spring again that night, and the next morning finished the last of their grub. Joe was getting a little out of hand at the inactivity as the day wore through, but later in the afternoon they saw a boy ride down the canyon and turn off into the brush and cedars near the spring.

They saddled their horses, and, leading them down the steep rimrock, surprised the boy, who was sitting back from the spring throwing pebbles into the water. A bunch of calves were munching grass nearby.

"Whatcha doin', kid?" Burt demanded gruffly.

"J-just openin' and shuttin' my eyes," the boy stammered.

Burt swung his rifle around in his direction. He actually did feel a little sorry for the frightened boy, but he didn't let on.

"We're hungry as bears," Burt explained. "We're going to get something to eat at your camp."

"We ain't got a thing," the boy said in obvious sincerity. "Mr. Childer is bringing back some grub tonight."

They helped him ease the batch of calves back into the pen. Most of them were branded with fresh markings. The boy admitted they had a hard time driving off the Hash Knife cows. His job was to water the calves and let them feed every afternoon, while the others did the branding.

It was twilight when all three started for the rustlers' camp. The boy was ordered to ride slowly ahead and told that he'd be killed if he gave any warning. The two men followed close behind, leading their mounts.

Burt and Joe were within a few feet of the campfire when the two rustlers, seated comfortably on a log, heard the words "Hands up!" They looked up into the muzzles of a pair of rifles that appeared to be as big as stovepipes.

The officers tied up the pair and stretched them out under a clump of brush. They were confident the boy would obey their orders without trouble.

It was almost dark when they heard the rattle of a wagon coming up the rough canyon trail. Childer and his companion rode straight into the trap. When Childer started to argue Burt cut him short.

"Shut up or I'll kill you!" he growled.

They were as hungry as wolves, so while Burt put ropes on them Joe dug into the grub sacks. They delayed starting until they cooked a meal. The boy fed the first two men who had been caught at the camp. Burt decided the last pair had eaten at their homes before they'd started back with the grub, so they didn't bother with them.

It was noon the next day when the wagonload of rustlers and the two men on horseback got to Holbrook. Within an hour Joe led Frank Wallace and a reliable witness back to the canyon and turned loose the freshly branded calves. They followed them until they located their mothers. Then they drove the bunch back to the county seat and put them in a corral. Several more witnesses were called in to see the calves, with their tell-tale brands, peacefully sucking the old Hash Knife cows.

Childer got three years at that fall term of court, and the other men two years each. The Hash Knife manager dropped a hint to the judge and the prosecuting attorney that it would be all right with him if the boy got off with a severe reprimand.

After all, he was just a kid. And that vile prison at Yuma would turn a boy into a criminal, if he wasn't one when he went there.

The people living in the towns and small communities along the Little Colorado were fairly well divided when it came to appraising Burt. The better elements, of course, were on his side, but there were still the tough, frontier groups that were violently allied against him.

It was pretty well accepted by both factions that sooner or later he would be killed. There were too many gun-toters like Bill Young still loose, and one of these days Burt's luck would forsake him. Time and the percentage were against him. And every man whom he had sent to Yuma swore he'd get him.

Burt was quite willing to accept the situation but he was a bit taken back when he found that Joe Bargeman's brother Ed was a sort of in-and-out leader of the people who opposed him. The man wasn't a bad sort of fellow when he was sober, but as soon as he was loaded he seemed to nurse a violent hate against the Hash Knife superintendent. Burt couldn't begin to explain it.

One Saturday afternoon Burt bumped into Ed on the sidewalk in front of the Bucket of Blood saloon.

"God damn you, get out of my way!" Bargeman swore. "I've taken all the insults from you I'm going to take!"

Burt was coiled to tangle with him, but he pulled himself up. He wasn't going to kill Joe Bargeman's brother. Without a word he stepped aside and walked on down the street.

The local toughs immediately hailed Ed as their new hero. At last someone had cussed out the great Burt Mossman to his face and got away with it! Ed Bargeman, they swore, had bluffed him, and Burt had taken the tongue-lashing and slunk off.

Toward evening Frank Watton ran into Burt in the drugstore. The sheriff called him to one side.

"Joe was just talking to me," Frank began. "He said to tell you that anytime you got in a row with Ed when he was drinking, you'd better kill him."

"Why, he's Joe's brother!" Burt answered.

"That's right, too. But Joe said to take no chances with Ed, and if you have to kill him it would be all right with him."

"Well, by God! What do you think of that!" was all that Burt could say.

He'd never figured that the deputy thought that much of him.

Burt had pretty well stopped the organized rustling, but he never could quite wrestle down Bill Young. The renegade lived back from Joe City, on north of the Little Colorado. He was off Hash Knife property, but he'd planted his little outfit in the midst of company cattle that ranged all year for miles above the Santa Fé tracks.

He had a neat trick of cutting the block of hide that carried the Hash Knife brand right out of an animal's side; and then sewing the open ends together. It made a mean-looking scar that was proof enough of stealing, but it wouldn't stand up in a court of law.

Most of the cow thieves who blotched brands ran a chance at detection. It was often impossible to be dead sure of a changed brand by merely looking at it; but when a critter was skinned and the hide examined on the inside the original brand was clear and unmistakable.

Young boldly ran his own brand on animals that bore the great scars where the Hash Knife mark had once decorated their left sides. Burt twice had him arrested and tried in the courts, but each time Young managed to beat the case.

When he was acquitted at the end of the second trial, Young passed out the word that he had had enough of persecution by Mossman and his Hash Knife brigands, and that he was moving to Colorado. For some reason the taunt didn't make Burt mad, and he walked up to the big fellow in a good humor.

"Bill," he began, when they were alone, "you and me been fighting one another for the best part of two years. Mind if I give you a little friendly advice?"

Young nodded for him to go ahead.

"When you leave this country leave your reputation behind. You've got boys growing up and a good wife. Go straight on account of them."

But Bill couldn't quite make the grade. Not more than a couple of years after he'd driven his little batch of two hundred mixed cattle, with their worked-over brands and scarred hides, up to Rifle, Colorado, word about him drifted back to Arizona.

He'd killed a man in a row and he and his oldest boy had been sent to prison for twenty years.

-- 7 --

Early in 1900 Burt got his orders to liquidate the last of the Hash Knife's fluid holdings. That spring and early summer he and Frank Wallace sent out their two wagons, and combed every square mile of the vast country their cattle roamed over.

In a way it was a repetition of his final days at both the Monticello and the Bloody Basin outfits. He seemed doomed forever to be closing out ranches. He'd never had a chance to show what he could do with an outfit that wasn't handicapped by drouths, or blizzards, or untamed ranges, or panic prices.

Someday, he swore, he'd show the world that he could build constructively, as well as liquidate successfully. He had a few thousand dollars saved, but it wasn't a tenth enough to start a real spread of his own. When he was still at the Bloody Basin he'd sold the Monticello ranch real estate for $2,000, which was $1,000 less than he'd paid for it. And, to add insult to injury, he never received a penny from the sale.

His dream of owning his own ranch would still have to be kept on ice. In the meantime, he'd find something interesting to do.

Mossman hadn't changed much in regard to his ambitions since he had been a boy. He was eager to make money and someday be classed as a rich man, but deep down within him the thing he hungered most for was life itself. He wanted to live in an exciting, colorful way; to stake his years on long shots, with the odds standing heavily against him.

He didn't think it all out, but it pleased him to feel that he'd already become somewhat of a man of distinction, a rather unique figure who was welcome in the company of the important and picturesque leaders of the Territory. It meant a good deal to him to be pointed out as Burt Mossman, the man who had conquered the tough Hash Knife outfit, and was going places.

But that was only part of it. He wanted to tell stories, and laugh and enjoy his gargantuan jokes, and give his sense of humor all the slack it could take.

With the work of cleaning up the tail end of the stock almost completed, Burt turned the active management over to Frank Wallace and took the train for Phoenix. He'd pretty well worn out himself riding the Hash Knife ranges and battling the rustlers night and day. He had already sent the directors his resignation, and he was ready for new worlds to tackle.

The first man he ran into at the Palace was the unique Colonel Bill Greene, who was sending the copper gamblers of Wall Street into a high sweat with his Cananea mine in Sonora. The Colonel ordered whiskey, while Burt took a cigar.

The tall, brash operator told Burt that he'd heard he'd been doing fine work up on the Hash Knife shipping his rustlers off to Yuma. "But you don't know nothin' about real hard hombres, Mossman," he added. "We got border half-breeds and Gringo outlaws so tough you couldn't kill 'em with a meat axe."

The Colonel was in an expansive mood as he reared back, his instep in the brass rail and his strong fingers gripping the curved edge of the mahogany bar. "Any day you want to tie into some real ones come on down and run my outfit for a while," he roared. "I got around thirty thousand head of cattle, and about half that many rustlers."

"Thanks, Colonel," Burt answered with a broad grin. "But I'm going out of the rustler business. There's about twenty hard nuts over in Yuma right this minute who are counting the days until they can get out and fill me full of lead. I'm a peace-loving man, Colonel."

Burt ordered another round. While the bartender was filling the order, Ed Tovrea joined them.

Tovrea was quite a figure along the border and up through Arizona. The story was that he was part French, with a dash of Mexican and maybe a little Italian thrown in. He weighed better than 250 pounds and he stood a good six feet in his stocking feet. He was big as a horse and tough as a mule; a strange mixture of generosity, reckless living and business acumen.

One time in a barroom fight he had been shot through the right hand, and the bullet had ripped up his arm, cut in between two cords in his neck and finally buried itself in his back. But it didn't slow him down.

In answer to a question from Colonel Greene he explained that he was about to enlarge his butcher business to include shops in Bisbee and Douglas, as well as Phoenix and Jerome. Someday he wanted to open a real packing plant here in Arizona.

But there were more adventurous things to do this moment than to talk business. Greene led the way to the roulette wheel in the back of the big room. The promoter lost ten thousand before he quit. Tovrea and Burt just about broke even and a little later Burt made himself some money at the poker table. Those endless hours he'd spent learning the game from cowboys and Indians, with cartridges as poker chips were paying off good interest now.

Before he left Phoenix he had pleasant talks with Governor

Oakes Murphy, Colonel Randolph and Charley Shannon, and other intimates. Burt always stopped at the Adams Hotel, owned by his friend J. C. Adams who'd once been a prominent Chicago attorney.

All of them were anxious to know what Burt proposed to do when he'd wound up the Hash Knife. Burt would shrug his shoulders, Mexican style, and answer, *"Quién sabe."*

"Who knows" was just about as near as he was willing to prophesy.

Anyway, it would be his own time and life he was gambling with.

Burt was back at the Hash Knife headquarters, closing up shop and making out his final reports, when a boy rode in from the depot at Joe City with a telegram.

It was from Ed Tovrea. There was a chance to buy out the Overlock Brothers of Bisbee, and take over their slaughter-house and retail shops. Tovrea wanted Burt to go in with him as an equal partner. Together they could expand and build up a great meat business.

Burt wired that he'd meet Ed in Phoenix and talk over matters. He'd already sold the final remnants of the Hash Knife herds to the Babbitt Brothers of Winslow, who the year before had bought the cattle and range of the Arizona Cattle Company, with its famous AI Bar brand. He arranged for Frank Wallace to stay on with the new outfit.

He was through. He'd done his best. The letter of commendation and thanks he'd received from the directors was worth all the hardship and loyalty he had poured out.

He'd step now into another world. And he'd make it hum.

His initial job for the Tovrea & Mossman Company was to take the train for Ft. Worth and arrange for regular ship-

ments of fat, grain-and-cottonseed-meal-fed steers to the slaughter-house in Bisbee. It would be the first time southern Arizona
had a chance to bite into real prime beef.

He beat the initial carload to Bisbee by a matter of days. At
the time there was Texas fever-tick quarantine in the Territory
against Texas cattle, and prospects looked tough. But Burt got
busy with his old friends on the Cattle Sanitary Board. He
promised he would build a high, tight fence around the slaughter
pens, in the isolated draw below Bisbee. Everything he imported
would be unloaded directly from the cars inside the stockade, so
that there could be no question of contamination. He put up such
a strong argument that the Board told him to go ahead.

The many-sided enterprise excited Mossman's imagination.
He and Tovrea were men of bold dreams, and they let them
soar. In a few months they were operating new retail outlets in
both Nogales and Douglas, and a total of eleven in Bisbee alone.
Frank Proctor, Mrs. Bill Greene's foster father, had the big end
of the meat business in the booming mine town of Cananea, on
below the border from Nogales, and Burt contracted for the
larger part of his trade.

They were making money hand over fist. Every week they
slaughtered a carload of fat hogs, shipped in from Wichita.
Their grain-fed beef came in by the carload from Ft. Worth, and
in season they daily killed around fifty head of sheep and a
wagonload of lambs.

Burt on his own hook ran up a concrete store building in
Douglas, leasing the right to use half the wall of a bank building
at $50 a year. He eventually turned his investment at $13,000.
He was learning how to make real money.

The two partners worked hard, but they played hard, too. Burt
enjoyed the jingle-jangle-jingle of twenty-dollar gold-pieces in
his pocket, and he was always ready for a fight or a frolic. But
somehow the new friends he made always came out of the top

drawer. The run of professional gamblers and tinhorn sports, and even the boss hard-rock miners, didn't seem to interest him.

More and more he left the impression of being aloof. He didn't mean to, but he gave off a sense of superiority that the border riff-raff could not help but resent.

His wit was as quick as his draw. One evening he was sitting in the back of his office in Bisbee when the bell of the wall telephone started ringing. He answered it.

"I'd like to have you send me ten cents' worth of cat meat right away," the sharp voice at the other end of the wire pronounced.

It was five o'clock and the delivery wagons had all finished their rounds and been put up for the night. And, anyway, it sounded ridiculous to Burt.

"I'm very sorry, ma'am," he said in his most genteel voice, "but we are completely out of cat meat. We haven't killed any cats since Wednesday. Good day, ma'am."

The irate lady snapped that she was taking her account to the California market. But Burt didn't mind: they owned that shop, too.

For the most part the days were gay and exciting for the young business man who had spent so many of his years on lonely, far-away ranches. Life was still rather crude in this roaring mining town of Bisbee, with its floating population of ten thousand, but there was a lusty humor about it all. Phoenix, too, was easy-going and wide and open. Nobody really minded, for instance, if the old Confederate officer, Dave Poole, got well-likkered and, standing up in his rattly buckboard like a Roman charioteer, drove his team of ponies at the high gallop down the middle of the capital's streets, sounding off his rebel yells.

Old Dave seemed to fancy Burt. "I've killed more damnyankees than you got fingers and toes, but I like you," he bragged.

Sometimes the old fellow rode horseback into town when he

took on a load. And one afternoon Burt found his pony standing quietly in the outskirts, while the old rebel lay nearby, where he had slid out of the saddle. Burt dusted him off, got him back on his horse and sent him on his way rejoicing.

Burt and his partner enjoyed the endless competition of seeing which one could peddle the biggest tales of Bisbee's goings-on. Burt always liked his own story of how he was sitting at the private desk of Mike Cunningham, president of the Bank of Bisbee, one morning when one of the town's better-known painted ladies flounced up to the teller's window with a check on this particular bank. The clerk quietly explained that the man who'd signed the check didn't have an account there.

"You mean you ain't gonna pay me them twenty bucks?" she irately demanded.

The teller shook his head, and when she continued to rant he suggested she walk over to Mr. Cunningham's desk and ask him. Burt listened while the bank president repeatedly explained how the gentleman who had drawn the check on his bank did not have an account there, and consequently the check was no good.

The long ostrich plume on her purple Gainsborough hat fairly snapped as she dramatically tore up the bit of yellow paper. Her hands rested on her ample hips and she struck a pose that would have done justice to a Bernhardt.

"And to think," she sounded off, "just to think, that sonofabitch stuck me for breakfast, too."

Colonel Greene had taken such a shine to Burt that he kept dangling one fantastic proposition after another in front of him. But Burt was wise to the extravagant promoter. One month Greene would be all but broke, and the next month he would be floating high in millions of paper profits. Burt liked his swaggering, lusty manner, but he was leary of getting under his thumb.

One day the Colonel came to Burt with the proposition of going into partnership and buying the famous ranch and cattle of Colonel Henry C. Hooker, an old-timer who had come out from California in the latter Sixties and built himself a valuable property north of Wilcox. If Burt could buy the outfit, Greene would put up most of the cash and Burt could be the manager.

It was a little too attractive for him to turn down cold, so the first chance he had Burt rode over to the Hooker spread. In many ways it was the show place of all lower Arizona, and Colonel Hooker was getting old and he was ready to sell.

After a week of study and examination, Burt agreed on the figure of $40,000 for the ranch property itself. They also settled on a price of $15 a head for the cattle, the calves thrown in, but Colonel Hooker insisted that his book count of 12,000 head of cattle be accepted. Burt had ridden several days among the herd, and he was certain the figure was way too high. So the deal was off and Burt went on back to his butcher business in Bisbee.

The whole country was prosperous in these early McKinley-Roosevelt days. The previous November the hero of San Juan Hill had been elected Vice-President, to sit alongside the sedate and precise President McKinley. Things were booming.

But despite the copper that turned into gold, and calves that became big steers, and expanding irrigation projects, there was a blight settling over this fair Arizona land. Murder, thieving, cattle rustling, railroad and stage-coach robbery and constant outlawry was loose all along the border, and across the deserts and on up through the mountains.

"How about you organizing a company of Arizona Rangers and cleaning up things?" Governor Murphy proposed one day when Burt was calling on him at the capitol in Phoenix. "We need a hard-riding, sure shootin' outfit something like the Texas Rangers or the Mexican Rurales. You're the very man to head it."

Burt threw up his hands. "Governor, I'm just beginning to hit pay dirt for the first time in my life. Much obliged, just the same."

"But you can help us write the bill, anyway," the Governor insisted. "Get hold of Frank Cox and outline the sort of Ranger outfit we should have."

Burt agreed to do his best, and that evening he and Cox, head attorney in Phoenix for the Southern Pacific, were closeted in a room in the Adams Hotel until midnight. The document was later smoothed out and presented to the Governor, and on March 21, 1901, duly appeared in the office of the Territorial Secretary as Act No. 74 of the Laws of 1901.

It provided for a company of Arizona Rangers, consisting of one captain, whose salary was to be $120 a month; one sergeant at $75 a month and not more than twelve privates at $55 a month.

Burt figured that his helping prepare the bill would be the end of the business, as far as he was concerned. But he was mistaken. The next time he saw Colonel Randolph the railroad man sounded off that Burt ought to head up the organization. He must do it for Arizona.

Every time Burt met one of his old friends he had to go through the same denials and explanations: he couldn't possibly leave his new business; there were plenty of other good men: get one of them.

But the pressure grew. Colonel Greene, Charlie Shannon, J. C. Adams—one by one they turned the heat on Burt. No other man in the Territory had the reputation and the experience to do the job, they argued. What did it matter if he was making $1,000 a month and had plans for a great packing plant in Phoenix? Arizona was calling.

Finally the Governor sent for him. When Burt walked into the office he found all his closest friends quietly waiting for him.

"Write out your own ticket, Burt," the Governor kept repeating. "But we're not going to take no for an answer."

For an hour they pounded away at him. Finally he said: "I'd want to pick the men myself, and have sole hirin' and firin' privileges."

"You've got my word that you can have anything you want that's in my power," Governor Murphy pledged.

Burt made one more provision: "I'll not stay more than a year, and I want the right to pick my successor."

The Governor jumped to his feet and gripped Burt's hand. The others crowded around and showered him with their thanks.

"Remember, it's only for a year," Burt kept repeating.

As a matter of fact, he seriously doubted if he'd last the year out. He was going against the toughest bunch of outlaws and thieves in the world. And he'd have exactly twelve men to fight a thousand—or maybe it was five thousand.

That made the odds an easy hundred to one against him. Which he figured was just about right.

Part Four

Ranger Captain

MOSSMAN had never killed a man. He had been in several gun fights and he had exchanged considerable hot lead, but he had never actually killed a man.

He had never wanted a reputation as a gun-fighter. In his long battle with the rustlers and outlaws of the Hash Knife country, he was perfectly willing to let it be known that he was hard and remorseless. But he shied from the questionable fame of being a killer.

He had rubbed elbows with too many men who could never escape the legends that pursued them. Few men could survive the competition and the jealousies that seemed to be connected with the successful gun-fighter.

Burt wanted none of it, but he was fully aware that his job of organizing and leading a company of Arizona Rangers left him no alternative but at times to "kill first and serve your warrant afterwards." He knew perfectly well when he took the job that he would be going against the most desperate gangs of outlaws and murderers in the southwest. There would be plenty of men killed, and Burt wasn't at all sure that he wouldn't be one of them.

He would have exactly twelve men to clean up a Territory that was almost as large as the combined areas of Ohio, Indiana and Kentucky. Roughly one-half of the country was mountainous and the other half desert. Most of the outlawry spread over the eastern part of the territory, centering around the headwaters of the Blue and Black Rivers in the north, and the Sulphur Springs and San Pedro Valleys to the south.

Oddly enough, in the northeast he would have to deal largely with Americans seeking refuge in the mountains after depredating in Utah, Colorado, Texas and New Mexcio. He was familiar with this country and this type of badman.

In the south he would operate in a district less familiar to him, and mostly against Mexicans and border outlaws. Of necessity his men would usually travel alone or in pairs. And they would have to be gun-fighters of great bravery and resourcefulness.

The first man he picked was Dayton Graham, a peace officer in Bisbee, whom Burt knew to be trustworthy. He made him his sergeant. The second man was Burt Grover, a lean, hard Texan who at times filled Graham's post. The third Ranger was named Leonard, and Burt chose him despite the fact that he had a brother who had been a member of the Burt Alvord gang, and at the time was serving a long sentence in Yuma for train robbery.

As each man was sworn in he was cautioned to tell absolutely no one that he was a Ranger. From the start Burt realized that his surest chance of success hinged on secrecy and surprise. The outlaw world had its own system of spies and accomplices, and to be effective this little band of officers would have to strike swiftly and silently on all its missions.

When the roster was filled Burt called the men into his headquarters office in Bisbee that he shared with Judge Starr Williams, a local J. P. It was a proud little outfit that he addressed on this first roll-call.

"We're thirteen, all told," he began. "And that will be an

unlucky number for a lot of outlaws. I'm not going to burden you men with a long list of instructions; if I didn't fully trust each of you I wouldn't have chosen you.

"Our first problem down here in lower Arizona is to break up the gangs moving in and out of Sonora, and using the Sulphur Springs and San Pedro Valleys as open highways for their cattle stealing and murdering. I consider it an armed invasion against our country when a bunch of Mexicans cross the border into Arizona."

Burt let his words sink in. Then he went on slowly: "I think these gangs should be treated exactly as you'd treat any other armed invaders. I'm going to leave it up to you just how you handle the matter. But I want to make one thing clear: whatever you do I'll stick to you. I'll back you to the hilt."

He made no formal division of his little company, but it worked out that usually there were three or four men working in the rough hills around St. Johns, northeast of the Fort Apache Reservation, while the rest were busy along the border. He tried to have one or two men at Bisbee as a sort of central reserve, ready and alerted for instant service.

Through his old friendship with Colonel Randolph, of the Southern Pacific, and with the Santa Fé people, his Rangers and their horses were given free transportation anywhere over these lines. In an emergency a special train would be thrown together and dispatched within an hour to any part of the Territory. These swift, silent tactics of surprise doubled the efficiency of the outfit.

One- and two-man patrols were immediately started out along the border, but the first real action fell to a small group of Rangers operating in the northeast. Word was flashed to headquarters at Bisbee that the post-office in Tucumcari, in eastern New Mexico, had been robbed and that a boy bystander, who had his hands up, had been killed. The outlaws, headed by one Bill

Daniels, had ridden westward, crossing the Rio Grande somewhere below Albuquerque.

Captain Mossman with four Rangers hurried by special train to Clifton and, unloading their horses, rode north to the rough country around the headwaters of the Blue. He posted his men in pairs on the most likely trails and sent word to the few isolated ranches and tiny settlements to be on the lookout.

The tip came shortly that a gang of five strangers were seen making camp. Mossman and his Rangers quietly closed in and at dawn surrounded the camp. Witt Neil and Roberts were captured in bed, and although Frank Lesseber and August Gibbon managed to escape, they were later shot to death from ambush. The fifth man of the gang, J. W. Smith, alias Sam Bass, was eventually captured.

Along with the bag of outlaws went a muleload of ammunition, high-powered Winchesters, heavy wire-cutters and ample grub, that came in mighty handy for the Rangers.

It was a fine start for the little company. Mossman still refused to give out the names of his troopers involved, and he was cagey about the whole operation. But the news of this mysterious and silent band of avengers quickly spread over the Territory. Here was something new and deadly for the law-breakers to think about. Desperate men who had long ridden with impunity, quietly questioned one another concerning this secret group that called themselves Rangers. They could learn little except that Burt Mossman, the tamer of Hash Knife rustlers, had organized the company and was their captain. But within three weeks the desperadoes were grinning as they heard of a sudden reversal of affairs.

Early in October Mossman had ridden into Solomonville from a scouting trip, to find a telegram awaiting him. It was signed by Henry Huning, a storekeeper and sheepman at St. Johns, and it contained the information that Bill Maxwell, one of the Rangers, had been killed in a fight with the Bill Smith gang at the headwaters of the Black River. Carlos Tefio, a second Ranger, was critically wounded. The third Ranger had gone for help.

While Mossman and the single Ranger with him were getting their horses ready for the long ride to Clifton and then on north, a second wire reached him. It read: "Tefio died from wound send force if possible up Blue to Mrs. Smiths place near Harpers Mill site she is mother of one of the murderers."

Burt and his Ranger made Clifton that afternoon, and the next day rode north at dawn. It was almost night when they pulled up at the forks of the Black River, some forty miles south of St. Johns, where the fight had occurred. Burt found Henry Barrett, an old rancher friend who had accompanied the three Rangers and had taken part in the scrap. Mossman got the story straight from him.

The Bill Smith gang had robbed a U. P. train in Utah and then headed south with a bunch of stolen horses. A rancher tipped off Barrett of his suspicions of the gang, and Barrett contacted the three Rangers. They swiftly organized a posse of a half-dozen cowboys and surprised the outlaws in their camp as they were skinning a bear. In the early exchange of shots Ranger Bill Maxwell was bored squarely between the eyes.

Finally Ranger Carlos Tefio shouted to the outlaws that they were completely surrounded, and would be annihilated if they did not surrender. Bill Smith, their leader, rose and with his hands raised above his head, started toward Carlos, asking where his men should come to give themselves up.

Carlos, thrown off his guard, stood up and directed Smith to lead them, unarmed, close to him. At that second Smith appeared to stumble and fall. Before Carlos knew what had happened, a shot tore through his intestines. The wily leader had dragged a rifle along by the toe of his boot hooked under the carrying strap.

When he pretended to stumble he had grabbed the rifle and shot.

Carlos, who lived in St. Johns and was one of the two married men in the Ranger company, gamely emptied his Winchester. Then he crawled to heavy brush where his horse was tied and collapsed. One outlaw was shot through the foot and another through the leg.

With the coming of night the outlaws escaped on foot, the posse having cut them off from their horses and camp supplies. The following morning the posse tried to follow the trail, but shortly they lost it. It was evening of that day when Mossman arrived.

Ranger Carlos Tefio had breathed his last around noon. While he was still conscious he called Henry Barrett close to him and managed to work his hand into his pants pocket and bring out a silver dollar. He handed this to Harry.

"Give this dollar to my wife," he whispered. "It, and the month's wages coming to me, will be all she'll ever have."

When Harry told Mossman the story, Burt asked him to turn the dollar over to him. "I've got something special I want to do with it," was his only explanation.

As soon as Mossman heard the full account of the fight, and examined the point where the trail was lost, he dispatched a Ranger to the Sam Carlos Agency with the request that the agent loan him Old Josh and one other Apache scout.

It was toward noon the next day when Josh showed up with a weazened little man, wearing big, oversized cowhide boots. He was called The Kid. Josh himself was fifty and was credited with being the best trailer among the Apache scouts. Years before, he had been sent out with instructions to bring in a renegade Indian, no matter how long it took him. Weeks passed and one day Josh came into Agent Crum's office carrying a sack. Without a word he emptied it on the table and a human head rolled out. Josh had had a little trouble fulfilling his mission but he'd finally brought in the proof.

Cap Mossman sent a lone Ranger south with orders to get men and guard the valley routes into Mexico, while he and his two Apaches tried to pick up the cold trail of the outlaws. His scouts cut sign late that afternoon and they followed the tracks up the Blue Mountains, that sprawled between the San Francisco and the upper waters of the Gila. There had been a snowfall and the clear trail led straight down to the isolated ranch of Hugh McKean.

The five men had been there the previous day. They had come in on McKean just as his wife was making supper. After taking all of McKean's weapons they helped themselves to his best horses and saddles. Then they sacked most of his grub and rode off toward New Mexico.

Mossman and his two Apaches hurriedly ate a meal before they took up the trail. Soon a heavy snow wiped out the tracks and for several days they floundered hopelessly. Their grub was running short, but Cap gave strict orders that the two Apaches should not shoot at game for fear the sound might warn the outlaws.

But when a grizzly broke out of a woods and lumbered across a clearing, the temptation was too strong for Mossman. He knew his first shot hit it in the back because he could see a puff of dust rise from the heavy hair. He let loose with two more slugs before the bear crossed a creek and disappeared in a clump of young oaks that covered two or three acres.

The three men cautiously walked around the area but they could find no tracks leading from it. Burt was certain the grizzly was still in the woods, and he told the two scouts to run it out while he took up a commanding position on a little knoll where he could kill it. The Apaches stubbornly refused. It was bad medicine for an Apache to kill or eat a grizzly, because the spirit of evil Indians entered a bear.

"We kill bronco man but not bronco bear," Old Josh kept repeating.

Burt offered them $10 each but they still refused. Then he called them cowards and finally told them he'd go in himself.

The trail was so clear he could have followed it on horseback. He stepped out gingerly and was half through when on ahead he caught sight of the great animal lying down. Its thick brown hair was waving suspiciously in the breeze when he shot.

He waited and when there was no movement, he closed in. The big animal was dead as a doornail when he reached it. His first shot apparently had given it the death wound.

Old Josh and The Kid were immensely proud of him. They told him that from now on they wanted to do the fighting. He must let them do the close-in work. They even demonstrated how the Apaches fought.

Old Josh threw his heavy cap fifteen feet to his right. Then he went through the motions of quickly raising his rifle and firing straight in front at some imaginary enemy. "Pow-pow!" he shouted, at the same instant rolling in the opposite direction.

Again he performed his deceptive trick of throwing an object to one side and at the moment an enemy might expose himself to steal a look, firing and then rolling in the opposite direction. "Me kill bronco man," he repeated. "You good man; you stay out."

A fresh snowstorm finally drove the three back to the McKean ranch. They had been almost three weeks on the trail and they had failed to catch their game. Mossman was certain that part of the gang with Bill Smith had cut south toward the Mexican border, so he paid off his scouts and returned to Bisbee.

He had two missions in mind. The first had to do with one Colonel Emilio Kosterlitzky, a legendary figure who commanded the Rurales of northern Sonora. Kosterlitzky had once been a Polish officer in the Russian army, and had been cashiered for some minor irregularity and subsequently had joined the United States army as an enlisted man. The story went that he had deserted at Ft. Bliss, near El Paso, and joined up with the famous Rurales, or Rural Guards, that had been established by President Porfirio Díaz from former outlaws who had accepted the government's proposition of either becoming peace officers or being shot.

In temperament and training Kosterlitzky fitted perfectly into the organization, and before many years he was put in command of all the Rurales in the upper half of Sonora. Tall, powerful, with long, black mustaches and flashing dark eyes, the Colonel dealt out his own brand of Rurale justice. He had no hesitancy in serving as judge, jury and executioner. Nor did he balk at the familiar device of the *"ley de fugar,"* or law-of-flight, whereby a prisoner being moved would be tipped off to attempt escape at a certain point. When he did so, he was promptly killed. The law-of-flight had double-crossed him.

Mossman had previously met the Colonel in the border town of Naco, and he now dispatched one of his Rangers there with the request for a conference at Bisbee. Within an hour after they met they reached a most important decision. Upon request the Rurales were to arrest and turn over to the Rangers any American in Sonora who was wanted. Mossman, in turn, promised that his men would apprehend and deliver to the Rurales any Mexican, living in Arizona, who was wanted by them. It was further agreed that when absolutely necessary either Rangers or Rurales could cross the border into the other's country in search of their own nationals.

It was strictly a gentleman's agreement, and it was observed in letter and spirit. No longer could Americans commit crimes on the American side and escape with impunity to privileged sanctuary below their own border. Nor could Mexican outlaws continue to steal and murder below the line and then gallop to safety above the border.

The two leaders drank a toast to their new arrangement and to one another's health. There was complete trust and confidence between them.

"By the way, *Coronel mío,* what has happened to that *bandido* Augustin Chacon?" Mossman quietly questioned. He was the man Cap was after more than all the others put together.

The Colonel shrugged his shoulders. "He is a bad one, *amigo mío.* We have not run into him for a year. I think he hides in the mountains in lower Sonora."

The Rurale chief pulled at his mustaches. "May I offer one word of advice, *Capitan* Mossman? It has paid us well to build up a network of spies. When they help us we forgive these informers their own little, what you call it—indiscretions."

Mossman thanked him and listened carefully while he elaborated on how he planted his spies and fences over his territory. "The dance-hall girls are especially good," the Colonel explained. "They seem to know almost everything."

Burt did not forget that odd bit of advice.

The second mission Mossman had set for himself called for a trip to Phoenix. Governor Murphy welcomed him and listened carefully to his report on the killing of the two Rangers, and on his long and unsuccessful trailing of the Smith gang.

Suddenly Burt reached in his vest pocket and pulled out a silver dollar and quietly explained how the dying Ranger Tefio had asked Harry Barrett to give it to his widow.

"This dollar and his month's pay is every cent the widow will have," Burt said slowly. "Governor, I want you to go before the Legislature and ask for a pension of $45 a month for that poor woman. We can't let her starve. She's our special responsibility."

Burt's eyes were swimming in tears and the Governor wasn't doing much talking. Within the hour the two men made their joint plea to the proper committee called in special session. They didn't try to check their emotions.

The committee chairman swallowed hard when he pushed through a bill to grant the pension. A little later it was steam-rollered through the Territorial Legislature and duly signed by the Governor.

On his first visit Mossman made to St. Johns he called on the widow and gave her the silver dollar.

He did quite a job of stammering when he tried to tell her about the pension.

-- 2 --

The loss of the two Rangers, and particularly the treacherous killing of Carlos Tefio, was a distinct shock to the little company.

"Take no chances with these buzzards," Mossman warned each of his men when he met up with them. "I'm not going to ask you why or how come you had to kill a man. All that I want is to make sure that you boys don't get killed yourselves."

It was a new point of view and an entirely revamped philosophy of gun-fighting for Burt. What he was really telling his men was not to give the other fellow much of a chance, but if he looked dangerous to kill him first and ask questions afterward. He had been brought up to be fair and just, and to ask for not more than a fifty-fifty break. But that even-Stephen stuff wouldn't work when it came to a handful of Rangers, operating alone or with only one or two mates in a vast, rugged country where every advantage lay with the outlaws.

Mossman and his men must learn to be as tough killers as the men they fought. The disaster of the Smith engagement had led the bandits to believe that it was comparatively easy to outshoot and outsmart the Rangers. Already the peace officers had lost the protection and advantage their anonymity had once given them. The outlaw underground had quickly spread the word of their individual identity.

Cap Mossman took to the saddle, working harder and taking more chances than any of his men. He had just returned to Bisbee from a long scout along the border when a wire arrived with the information that the paymaster of the Calico mines had been shot out of his buckboard, and his payroll in gold coin taken while he was crossing a lonely strip of desert.

In less than an hour Cap and his only available Ranger were riding hard to the south. The two men found the abandoned buckboard, but others had been there and it was impossible to be sure of the bandit's trail. Burt and his man separated. Each would ride alone, doubling the long chance of cutting sign and then following the trail at top speed.

It was a waterless, forbidding land, marked with giant saguaro and clumps of Spanish bayonet, yet it bore the lovely name of Paradise Valley. Burt was sure he was on the right trail and he followed it as fast as he dared push his mount.

Suddenly he caught sight of a riderless horse standing motionless, with its head dooping low. He figured that the animal had been ridden to complete exhaustion and then abandoned. He could make out the tracks of man on foot, off to the right.

They led straight toward a water-hole that was in reality a swamp marked with clumps of rushes and Spanish bayonet. Burt pulled his rifle from its boot, and threw a shell in the breech. He was positive his man was hidden somewhere within this acre or two of morass. His grey-blue eyes narrowed to slits as he searched for sign.

Suddenly a bullet knicked the flesh of his right leg, as the sound of the explosion split the silence, and the ghost of a tiny whiff of smoke appeared straight ahead. He caught a suspicion of movement at the base of a clump of brush.

He jerked his rifle to his shoulder and quickly aimed, and fired. Then he slid from his horse and waited.

There was no second shot. Cautiously he approached the spot he had aimed at. His single shot had been a lucky one. The slug had torn off the top of the man's head.

He was a Mexican, and Mossman carefully searched his pockets. A letter proved that his name was Salivaras. Next to Augustin Chacon he was the most famous Mexican bandit and Gringo-killer operating along the border.

It was easy to piece together what had happened. After waylaying the paymaster he had pushed his horse too hard, and when the animal had failed him he had taken the bag of gold coins and sought refuge in the swamp. He had tried to dig a hole in the mud and hide himself and his loot. When Mossman had ridden up within a hundred yards the bandit was certain he would be seen and he had taken a shot at him. It had only snipped the peace officer's leg. Mossman's fine shot had been his end.

Burt left the body, but tied the bag of money to the pommel of his saddle. He retraced his steps at a walk, for his own mount was suffering from heat and thirst.

He had a good deal to think about. It meant something to kill a man, even if he had done it in self-defense. Certainly the man needed killing, for he had robbed and butchered Americans and had never given any of his victims a fair chance for his life.

This Salivaras was a good start. But it was only a start. There were scores of other outlaws, almost as dangerous. One at a time they'd have to be run off, captured or killed.

And always there would be the murderer Augustin Chacon as his final goal.

Morale was going up in the Ranger company. Burt had many applicants for the vacancies of the two men lost, but he acted cautiously. For one thing he decided to take on new men only after a period of probation.

He still had one vacancy open when a tall young Texan came into his headquarters office in Bisbee. He looked the money, although Cap Mossman realized that he was probably on the dodge. He said that his name was Wheeler and admitted modestly that he was good with a rifle and six-shooter, and knew horses and how to cut sign and was familiar with the various arts of frontier life.

Mossman was just leaving on a long scout that would take him below the border into the Spur Mountains. He fixed the boy up with a horse and equipment and took him along. It was two weeks before they returned, but Cap had himself a new Ranger.

Through the grapevine that ran straight to the red light district of Bisbee, Cap was tipped off that there would soon be a holdup in the Legal Tender saloon and gambling hall in Tucson. He decided he'd find out what his new boy could do on his own.

Cap told him to take the train to Tucson but not to go into the saloon until midnight. He was to speak to no one and quietly post himself with his back against the wall where he could keep his eye on the faro game. The room was at least a hundred feet long and Wheeler was to stand about half-way down from the front door.

"And just one thing more," Cap concluded. "I'm tired of you fellows sending me windy telegrams as long as love letters. I have to pay most of the incidentals of this outfit out of my own pocket, so keep your telegrams down to ten words. Understand— exactly ten words."

Two mornings later Cap was having breakfast in a little restaurant just over the bridge. He saw a boy come out of the Western Union office on the trot. He had a hunch the lad had a wire for him so he called out of the open window to him. His hunch was correct, and he tore open the yellow envelope and took out the sheet. It read:

"One man holdup Legal Tender two am inquest four pm." It was signed "Wheeler."

Mossman grinned as he counted off the words. The Ranger had neatly kept within the ten-word limit.

The next day when he got back he told Cap how he'd followed his instructions and posted himself half-way down the wall, near the faro game. Shortly before two o'clock, the hour when the proprietor locked up the big end of the night's take in the safe, a man pushed through the front door and, pulling a gun, shouted "Hands up! Everybody put 'em up!"

Wheeler's first bullet entered his heart just below his left nipple. His second shot lodged a little below the right nipple. The bandit was dead as a mackerel when he hit the floor.

In helping to write the bill that brought the Rangers into existence, Mossman had failed to provide for the proper funds to pay for the endless list of minor incidentals that kept cropping up.

Purely as a matter of following the line of least resistance Cap simply paid for the extras out of his own pocket and forgot it.

He had already fallen into the habit of telling the Governor only such reports of routine fights and Ranger operations as he felt he should know about. It did not seem necessary to over-shock the chief executive with constant recitals of the many grim little battles.

But, oddly enough, Burt began to feel that he himself was being cheated of certain details by his own men. Now and again there would come to his ears, as well as to the Governor's, fantastic reports of entire bandit gangs cut down and annihilated. Burt knew that rumors had a way of doubling in size at each retelling, but they did get pretty big.

Then, too, he believed that some of the small bills his boys were charging to him, and which he was paying for out of his own funds, were not always necessary. One of his men, for instance, dropped into the headquarters at Bisbee after a prolonged scout with three other Rangers over in the Sulphur Springs Valley. Cap had just opened a bill from a hardware company in Douglas for two shovels, and he was put out about it.

He greeted his man, who rather apologetically reported that he and his companions had caught a little gang of Mexicans driving a stolen batch of cattle toward the border and they had settled with them.

Before he asked for further details Cap Mossman handed the man the bill for two shovels. It was marked $2.70.

"Is that bill correct?" Cap demanded.

"Yes, sir."

"Well, what in hell did you have to have two shovels for?"

The Ranger slowly shook his head. "Honest, Cap," he pleaded. "There was seven of them sonsabitches and one man just couldn't do all that diggin'."

-- 3 --

Cap was lucky to have three Rangers with him at Bisbee when the wire came from Yuma. It wasn't signed but Cap knew who sent it. The chief cattle buyer in Yuma was a friend of his and Cap had told him to keep his eyes and ears open, and when he heard anything the Rangers should know to tip him off.

The wire was a bit cryptic but Cap made it out: six suspicious Americans were denned up twenty miles below the border on the Colorado River. Cap studied the various sheriff notices pinned on his bulletin board. Sure enough, there was one from Utah regarding six train robbers who had headed south.

Cap called up Colonel Randolph's office and arranged for a special train of an engine, stock car and caboose. He had his men load their own horses, and late that afternoon they piled into the caboose and pulled out across the Arizona desert for the flat-roofed town of Yuma, on the extreme western border of the Territory.

They arrived just about daylight, and Cap ordered his men to put their horses in the cattle buyer's corrals, and then go straight to the hotel and keep hidden in their rooms. He went on ahead and had the hotel clerk send a boy with a message to the cattle buyer.

It was dark that night when Cap and his three men quietly rode south from the town. One of them led a little red packmule, with a sack of grub and a box of dynamite sticks strapped on his back.

They followed the muddy, steaming Colorado for twenty miles and at dawn pulled up in a heavy clump of brush and trees, and made what passed for a camp. Each man carried a small sack of oats for his horse and a little grub for himself. It was spring and warm enough to sleep out without a blanket.

Early afternoon Mossman mounted and riding alone swung in a wide arc southward, bending well to the east of the river. A couple of miles below the camp was the ghost town of Colonia, with a woman and her four brothers one of the few families still living there. Their herd of cattle ranged up and down the river, and the stock buyer in Yuma bought their beef, and was their friend. One of the brothers riding into Yuma for supplies had told him of the six mysterious Americans who were living in an abandoned house back from the river and not far from their own adobe. It was this tip that had been relayed on to Cap Mossman in Bisbee.

Keeping well to the east, Mossman rode quietly along, nursing his luck. Shortly he saw a lone Mexican horseman and headed toward him. He greeted the Mexican and when he learned his name, handed him a note from the cattle buyer. It was a request that every courtesy be shown the bearer, Captain Mossman.

The Mexican bowed that he was his *atento servidor.* He explained carefully that the six Americans were occupying the last house next to the river. His own house was fifty yards or so to the east. No, the men posted no guards at night. They played cards and then the candles were put out and all was quiet.

"There is just one request I would like to make," Cap Mossman finally said. "Will you keep all your dogs inside your house tonight?"

The Mexican promised, and Cap thanked him and they parted.

Back at the camp Cap explained to his men what he had found. They would start out an hour before dawn. They'd better leave the red mule tied up here, for his braying might betray them. They could ride their horses part way and carry the dynamite themselves.

One of the three Rangers had once been a hardrock miner's helper and he understood explosives. While it was still light Cap had him divide the sticks into four equal parts, and have each batch laced together. Carefully he clinched each cap to a fuse and then shoved it into the side of a stick. The four fuses were cut exactly the same length.

The men left their horses a quarter-mile from the house, and walked forward as noiselessly as they could. Each man was ordered to place his sticks against the corner of the house. He was to light the fuse the instant Cap's match flared. Then he was to slip back toward the only door and choose his own firing position.

There was barely enough light to sight along a rifle barrel when Cap bent down over the end of his fuse and struck his match. Then he quietly picked up his rifle and tiptoed toward the

front of the house. Within five seconds all four fuses had been lit and the men were moving to their posts.

The explosions were almost simultaneous. Even though the house was made of adobe, with wooden vigas and dirt roof, it was shattered. The outlaws poured out like frightened rats escaping from a wire cage.

The uncertain light of the dawn, with the shock and excitement of the explosion, made fine shooting a bit difficult. One man of the six got away and ran for his horse near the river bank. It was always a matter of chagrin to Cap Mossman how he and his three men failed to score six straight bull's-eyes.

When full light came the Rangers searched the house ruins and the area along the river for the hidden loot of the train robbery. There were papers enough on the men to prove amply that there had been no mistake made.

But dig as they would, the peace officers could locate no cache of gold or bills or silver. The only money found was some $360 discovered on the bodies of the five dead men. Cap allowed it wasn't enough to bother turning in, so he had his three men divide it among themselves.

The Mexican vaqueros helped them dig the five graves, and Cap gave them the hobbled horses that the bandits had turned out to graze. The gift included the saddles and such equipment as had survived the explosion.

But it was not a completely happy little party that rode on north to Yuma late that afternoon. It didn't seem possible that four of the best rifle-shots in Arizona could have let that sixth man escape without a scratch.

It troubled Cap Mossman all the days of his life.

-- 4 --

Mossman and his men knew instinctively how important it had now become for them and their deeds to grow into legends in the minds of the public. So the stories spread of how well-known desperadoes would ride off on a foray and evaporate into space. Or how rustlers would start off from one side or the other of the border and never again be heard from.

Cap Mossman finally began to wonder if some of his men weren't almost a little too good at killing. He cautioned them to keep on shooting first, but to be fairly sure they were right. And if they were so anxious to prove their invincibility let them bring in the famous Chacon, or even Bill Smith. There was a report that the Ranger-killer had been seen along the border, and Cap insisted that he'd make a good enough meal for a couple of Rangers any time.

After the killing of Carlos Tefío and the emotional business of securing the pension for his widow, Mossman had stuck to his resolve to enlist no more married men. But Dayton Graham was still one of his best and most fearless Rangers. Graham had a wife and two children living in Bisbee, and Cap worried quite a little that sooner or later he'd be killed.

This was especially true after an incident that occurred one midnight on lively Brewery Gulch. Graham, stepping out from a bar, saw a man in the middle of the street, a few feet away, apparently in a very big hurry to mount his horse.

"Hello, pardner. What you doing here?" Graham questioned, walking toward the head of the horse.

In the dim street light he could see the man reach for his pistol. Graham ducked under the horse's head and the bullet missed him. His own shot tumbled the man out of his saddle. One slug was enough. He'd been right, too, in his hunch: the man had just finished sticking up a barroom.

After that Cap tried to give Graham some of the less dangerous assignments. He used him a good deal on patrolling the border around Douglas, with special instructions to keep his eyes peeled for both Chacon and Bill Smith. Cap had no picture of good Smith, but he was positive that sooner or later he would show up.

One evening Graham was chatting with Tom Vaughn, the night marshal, not far from the immigration station between Douglas and Agua Prieta. Suddenly a storekeeper walked up to them and said that there was a suspicious-looking man sitting on the porch in front of his store, a short distance down the street. The two peace officers strolled over to the building and approached the man.

"Good-evening, stranger. Are you lookin' for somebody?" Vaughn asked as a routine question.

For an answer the man whipped out a pistol and shot the night marshal through the jugular vein.

Graham had his pistol half-way out of its holster, when a slug tore through his right lung and a second shot hit his arm. The storekeeper ran from the scene while the murderer calmly joined a group of tourists trooping into the Mexican town and disappeared.

A telegram was immediately sent to Mossman at Bisbee with the news that Graham was dying. With heavy heart Cap ordered a fast team and hack, and then hurried to the home of the Ranger. Mrs. Graham dressed her children as quickly as she could, and Cap took the reins for the twenty-six-mile drive to Douglas.

It was well after midnight when they pulled up at an adobe house where the wounded Ranger was lying. His wife knelt by his bed but he pushed her away.

"I want to talk to Cap," he whispered. "I ain't gonna die."

They brought Cap into the room and he put his ear close to Graham's lips. "Don't worry, Cap," he said slowly. "I'll live to get that sonofabitch. He's got coarse black hair and his front teeth are wide apart. I'll know him."

Mossman quieted him down as much as he could; and back in the adjoining room assured his wife that he didn't think her husband would die. He had too much fight left, he insisted.

For two months the Ranger was bedridden, and during the last half of his medical sentence he was fit to be tied. A rumor was brought him that one Baylor Walton was reported to have said that Graham was well enough, but he was afraid to come downtown. He still was a little shaky when he dressed and strapped on his gun and left the house.

He located Walton and when the Ranger threatened him with death if he didn't take him to the man who had started the gossip, Walton led him to "Long Shorty," the new town marshal. The peace officer finally admitted he might have made the disparaging remark about Graham when he was drunk. He was sorry he had said it.

The incident apparently was ended, when "Long Shorty," morose and angry, took on a load and went gunning for Walton. The marshal found his prey seated at a table next to the cigar stand in a saloon. Just as the officer reached for his gun, the bartender shouted for Walton to look out. Walton threw himself back in his chair, drawing at the same instant. A lucky shot hit the drunken marshal squarely in the heart.

Walton, fearful of "Long Shorty's" friends in court, slipped across the border. A few days later his father came over from Texas and interviewed Mossman.

"Your son fired in self-defense," Cap assured him. "Have him come on back here and stand trial, and I'll assure you he'll be acquitted."

But the father could not get his son to return, and within a month or two a report drifted up from Mexico that he had been killed in a fight at Colonel Greene's mines in Cananea. It was the old story: he had failed to sustain his fame as a gun-fighter against jealous rivals. But the sorry drama of death still had its last act to be played.

Ranger Graham quietly went about his task of locating the man who had shot him. Nightly he drifted from one saloon and gambling hall to another, slipping through the red light districts on both sides of the border, looking for the man with the coarse black hair and the front teeth that were set wide apart. He asked Captain Mossman to be patient with him and give him no outside assignments. Mossman was beginning to feel his pet Ranger was spending a little too much time on his private feud, but he let him alone.

Then one night Graham saw his man seated at a monte layout. He wanted the outlaw to get a good look at the man who was about to even up the score. Graham let him start for his gun before he shot.

"You won't kill no more sheriffs, you bastard," Graham said quietly, as he put in two more slugs. Then he walked over to the police station and gave himself up. He was turned loose on his own recognizance, and the next morning when Cap Mossman arrived from Bisbee he had the whole thing wiped off the slate.

They found thin, steel hacksaw blades sewed in the collar of the outlaw's coat, and evidence to prove he was the Bill Smith they wanted.

It had taken quite a little time but the Ranger had finally squared up his own private account and, as well, the matter of the treacherous killing of poor Carlos Tefio.

It was a couple of weeks later that Cap Mossman heard two or three of his men talking over a raid they wanted to make on their own hook. It was to be on a tough old rancher who lived with his two grown sons on the west slope of the Chiricahua mountains, thirty or forty miles north of the border.

"That old cow thief does everything from stealing horses to making bootleg whiskey," one of the men remarked. "We ought to drop in there and clean him out."

Mossman raised his hand. He didn't think they had a single thing on the old fellow—except rumors. It could well be said that he was simply the victim of enemies down in the valley who were spreading tales against him.

"Why, Cap! That old man is as guilty as hell," one Ranger insisted.

Cap mildly explained that some of the good people of Arizona were beginning to think that the Rangers were getting a little too big for their britches. This was one case he'd handle himself. It seemed pretty clear to him that the rancher and his boys were being pushed into becoming outlaws. He'd go up there and do a little investigating on his own.

There was a small insurrection staged and his men insisted he take at least two of them with him. But Cap shook his head. He'd go alone, but if he didn't come back in three days, they could take a force up there and kill 'em all.

When Cap swung down from his horse and started for the door of the little mountain ranch house, he wasn't quite so sure about his judgment. A thin, slatternly old woman met him and motioned him to come inside.

"I want to talk to your husband, ma'am," Cap explained. "Is he home?"

"No, he and the boys are working stock on below," she answered.

Cap walked to the window and looked out toward the corrals. The woman was standing in front of the fireplace and when Cap turned around she had a double-barreled shotgun, that she'd grabbed off the mantel, pointed at him.

"You Yankee devil!" she rasped. "I reckon I better kill you right now!"

Cap was as frightened as he had ever been. This old rebel was full of fire and he'd have to talk fast.

He had just about dissuaded her when his horse gave himself a big shake, and a pair of handcuffs bounced out of his saddlebag. The woman saw them as they hit the ground.

"You'll never put them things on my menfolks!" she spat out. "You Rangers been killin' too many innocent people round here. It's time *we* did a little shootin'."

Fortunately at that moment the old man rode up. "What's the matter, Mother?" he questioned when he stepped into the house.

Burt talked for his life. He explained who he was and how he'd ridden out here alone because he felt that the reports he'd heard about the family were untrue. He didn't want any more killings on anybody's part.

"I want you and your sons to go to Bisbee with me," he went on. "I want you to face any charges that are against you and get them cleaned up. You've been outlawed for two years, and I got a hunch it's all wrong."

The old man was still a little skeptical. "Mister, you talk sense, but it's hard to believe you. We ain't done nothin' wrong, but we're always gettin' accused of it. Say, can we take our guns with us?"

"I'm carrying mine and you can pack yours."

A half-hour later the little party of four started on the long ride. When they got to Cap's office he unbuckled his belt and piled his gun, holster and rifle in a corner. He explained that while they were in town his three guests better do the same. One by one they followed suit.

Then Mossman led them to the judge's office and asked for a special hearing. In a matter of minutes the charges against them were heard and dismissed. Then Cap bought them something to eat, and a drink or two, and the three men strapped on their guns and started home.

Cap didn't mind how far this story about him spread.

-- 5 --

Early in the game Cap found out that it paid off for him personally to break in any new Ranger whom he had on probation. So it was that he happened to have one with him in Tucson when he got word of the murder there of a Mexican girl by two men. The brutal part of the outrage was that the fingers of the girl had been cut off so that her rings could be taken.

Cap had sources in the seamier side of Tucson's night life, and he did his own detective work. He found that the murderers were Mexicans and that they had left town by horseback only an hour before, and would probably try to cross the border at Sasabe, sixty miles to the south. There was no railroad or telegraph lines to the little border town.

The first twenty-five miles of the road was hard-surfaced at this time, and although it was impossible to cut sign Burt and his man rode rapidly toward Sasabe. By the time they reached the end of the hard road they could see dust rising ahead on the dirt road that indicated they probably were not far behind the pair.

To go straight on down the dirt road would stir up dust that might arouse the suspicions of the murderers. Off to the left was a line of hills and Mossman led the way through a fold to a trail that ran south along the east slope.

They were riding tough, grain-fed horses and they called on them for the best they had. Ten or twelve miles further on south a trail cut through a pass in the hills to the right, and led to the main dirt road. If they could reach this ahead of the Mexicans they could intercept them.

They drew up in a clump of brush and waited. Shortly they could see the pair riding toward them at an easy trot, oblivious to any danger. Mossman drew his pistol and held it concealed behind his saddle pommel. The young Ranger followed his lead.

They waited until the Mexicans were only a few rods up the road, when they suddenly appeared and threw down on the pair. The young Ranger rode in close and while Cap leveled his gun, he disarmed them. It took less than a minute to snap the handcuffs on their wrists held behind their backs, and to search their pockets. He found the stolen rings, with the dried blood still on them.

"What do you think?" Cap questioned grimly. "I'm so tired out I couldn't stay awake to guard these bastards."

"Neither could I, Cap," the young Ranger agreed. "You know, Cap, I ain't very smart but I got an idea."

He reached down and untied the buckskin string that held his rope on the right side of his saddle horn. Cap shook out his own rope.

In less than a minute each Ranger had his loop drawn around the neck of a prisoner, and catching up a bridle rein led the horses to the far side of the hills and into a heavy clump of trees. One of the Mexicans started to plead for mercy, but the second killer told him to shut up and die like a man.

Nothing more was said. Each Ranger tossed the end of his riata over a heavy limb of a tree that grew close to the edge of a cut-bank. Carefully measuring off the proper slack that would be needed, each tied his rope to the tree trunk.

Then at a nod from Cap they led off the bandits' horses. The doomed men swung out into space and dangled fantastically from the stout limb. Quickly the Rangers removed saddles and bridles and with a slap across their rumps sent the ponies galloping toward the border and home.

"Well, we saved the county a few thousand dollars in not having to try those sonsabitches," Cap allowed, when they were well started for Tucson.

They were several miles further along when he added: "Maybe

it's just as well for you and me to keep this as our own private little secret."

"Reckon you're right, Cap. But goddam, did you see them bastards kick?"

All this happened a half-century ago, at a time when violence could be matched only by violence.

-- 6 --

The days and weeks moved by with incredible swiftness for Cap Mossman. No sooner would he get one nasty job cleaned up than another presented itself.

He had determined from the start that he would be the real leader and that he would never send his men into any spot where he hesitated to go himself. He knew all along that his little company must be afire with esprit, and filled with its own sense of destiny, or it would have no chance to succeed. Already opposition was crystalizing against him, and a good deal of it was of a personal nature.

Even the sheriffs of Cochise and Santa Cruz Counties, along the border, were more or less jealous of him and his growing reputation. While they were too smart to oppose him actively and openly, they certainly did little actually to help him.

Most of the lower level of gamblers and saloon-keepers, along with the tough riff-raff, made no bones of their hatred for him. He was arresting, or extraditing, or sending off to Yuma—or plain killing—too many of their own kind. And they resented, too, his aloofness and his unconscious exclusiveness. He was seen too much with such high-toned men as Governor Murphy and

Judge Barnes and the other leaders of Arizona's fairly rough-diamond upper crust, and he made no effort to conceal how he despised tinhorns of all descriptions.

The French saying that "appetite grows with eating" was by no means reversed in Cap Mossman's case. From one end of the Territory to the other, he was now known as "Cap." Even his old friends who had long called him Burt, began addressing him with his military title. It did not displease his vanity.

He had done extraordinarily well for a young man just turning thirty-five. He had built on solid foundation his reputation as being possibly the best range and ranch manager in the whole Southwest. And now he was adding to that the distinction of being a Ranger captain who had no superior in the world as a thief-catcher and bandit-killer .

Now and again he would run into Colonel Bill Greene as the extravagant promoter shuttled in his private railroad car back and forth between New York and his Cananea properties in Sonora. The Colonel's greeting was always the same: "Cap, when you going to give up this Ranger job and go in with me?"

Burt would smile and shake his head. He still had a few more bad ones to pick off and then he'd resign.

"You keep a sharp eye out for a big ranch we can buy," Colonel Greene remarked the last time they met at Douglas. "Teddy Roosevelt will be appointing one of his old Rough Riders as Governor of Arizona one of these days, Cap, and you'll be out of a job. You better resign now and beat 'em to the punch."

"Wait till I get Chacon," Cap replied. "I'll quit then."

Ever since President McKinley had been assassinated, shortly after the Rangers had been organized, Mossman knew his days were numbered. Already Teddy was filling western offices with his beloved Rough Rider comrades. He'd get around to a new Governor for Arizona Territory one of these days. Greene was right, but Cap couldn't quit yet.

Ever since he was twenty-one Mossman had been handling hard men, but these Rangers of his were something else again. From the very nature of their dangerous work they had to be strong individualists and proud men. They traveled so close to the perpetual threat of violence and death that they couldn't help but be a little on the frisky side when they did let down. It took a master to know when to give them their heads and when to ride with a tight rein.

Early one morning Cap and four or five Rangers rode into the livery stable in Tombstone. They had just missed corralling a gang of rustlers, and Cap figured he might pick up fresh clues in the old mining town. He carefully instructed his men to stay hidden while he made a private contact or two.

He had already had a little trouble with one of his younger men named Ed Scarborough, who was a son of the late George Scarborough, one of the most efficient peace officers the Southwest had ever had. A year or two before this, George had died of wounds received in a gun fight he and Billy Burchfield had with five outlaws. The young Ed Scarborough was a bit on the harum-scarum side, and traveled quite a little on his father's reputation.

When Cap returned to the livery stable in Tombstone, he found that Ed had disobeyed orders and gone over to the courthouse and picked up a fight. The sheriff had grabbed him, but when he discovered that he was a Ranger he had turned him loose.

"You're under arrest," Cap said sternly.

The boy started for his gun and Mossman knocked him down. He almost fell under the heels of one of the horses, and he was lucky he didn't get kicked to death.

Cap sent him under guard back to the sheriff's office, with instructions that he was to be jailed until Cap got back.

The little party pointed into the mountains above Clifton on what was to be a short scout, but they were gone almost three weeks. In the meantime Ed Scarborough pulled every possible string to get himself out of jail. He even appealed to the Governor, but neither the Governor nor the sheriff would budge. If Cap Mossman said to hold the boy until he got back, that was what was going to be done.

When Cap finally did show up, he discharged young Scarborough from the Rangers, and sent him on his way. The boy drifted over to the San Pedro Valley and went to work for an outfit that Henry Street was running. It was the same Henry Street whom Mossman had known over in the Rio Grande country. It wasn't long until Ed killed a homesteader in a quarrel, and was sent to Yuma for life.

It was shortly after this little affair at Tombstone that Cap happened to be up around his old Hash Knife stamping ground at Holbrook. He was shocked one morning to get a wire from St. Johns, the county seat of Apache County, that his friend Sheriff Henry Beeler had been killed. He borrowed a good horse from his trusted pal Frank Wattron and started out at once.

Mossman had only meager details of the trouble that led up to the killing. Pete Slaughter, a first cousin of the famous John Slaughter, old border-rancher and one-time sheriff at Tombstone, had two sons, Monte and Pat. It seemed that Monte and Sheriff Beeler had had a fist fight over a card game. The sheriff had knocked Monte down, and the young man had quietly hurried home and come back with a shotgun.

The sheriff saw Monte as he passed by the window with his gun, and when he burst through the front door Beeler promptly killed him. It was clearly a case of self-defense.

Monte Slaughter's younger brother Pat, and a cousin, Mal Jewel, took up the Slaughter cause, and hiding behind a stone sheep corral that was built very close to the unmarked Arizona-

New Mexico line, shot the sheriff out of his saddle when he rode by a day or two later.

The two young men figured the officer was dead and they skipped off into the mountains. But the sheriff lived until four that afternoon and he was able to whisper the names of his two assailants.

On reaching the scene Cap immediately started out with one man. The second afternoon he cut fresh sign, and he followed the trail through the gathering twilight. When night dropped down he was sure he was not more than a mile or so from his quarry.

He tried to sleep, but he was afraid the two men might break camp at dawn and he would lose them. A slip of a moon did its best to cut through the darkness, but it helped little. This was country he had traveled over, hunting for both man and game, and he was fairly familiar with it. He awakened his companion, determined to try his luck despite the dark night. He had a hunch he'd find the pair in a grove of trees on the lip of a canyon, about a mile to the southwest. It was an ideal campsight for men on the dodge.

Suddenly a horse snorted, and a few moments later Cap caught the sound of men running. He made his way to the edge of the canyon. From down below he could hear the noise of crashing rocks and the popping of brush as if men were rapidly making their way down the steep, rocky slopes.

He found the hastily evacuated bed, and throwing back the tarp, struck a light. Crude letters blocked in red paint a foot high on the canvas spelt out the name PAT. That was proof enough that it belonged to Pat Slaughter. Cap had sprung the right trap but his prey had escaped.

For a week he tried to pick up the trail but he failed, and he was thoroughly disgusted by the time he got back to Holbrook. He had come so close yet missed so far.

Some months later Henry Grey, the third Ranger who had been in the Bill Smith fight in the early days of the force and had escaped being killed, ran into Pat Slaughter in Clifton and arrested him. The trial came off in the late fall of 1902, and the defense built its case on the premise that the prosecution must prove that the sheep corral, where the killing of Sheriff Beeler had occurred, was in Arizona and not over the line in New Mexico. It failed to do that and Pat got off.

Mossman always held that had he still been with the Rangers, he would immediately have sent up a registered surveyor and located the exact spot where the ambush had been set. He was certain it was on the Arizona side.

Burt Mossman had very little time these days for anything but business, but now and again he'd sit in at a poker game or buck the roulette wheel. He had made it a rule never to play cards with his own men, but he enjoyed a little session with friends whenever he could work one in.

The same was true with his hunting. When he was out on a long scout and fairly certain that the sound of a gun wouldn't tip off the presence of Rangers, he'd bring in a deer or a bear.

The snow was still deep in the mountains when he and Sheriff Jim "Hard Times" Parks did a bit of scouting-hunting together in the hills west of Clifton. They were coming into camp one night toward dusk when Cap saw grizzly bear tracks. He and Parks crawled out of their blankets at three the next morning, and turned loose their lone hunting dog. He led them for miles on foot but they never did catch up with the bear.

The men were all packed up and ready to leave when the hunters, pretty well tuckered out, got back to camp. There was hot bacon and coffee waiting for them and it kept them going until they reached Hugh McKean's ranch, where the Bill Smith gang had stolen horses and where Cap and his two Apache scouts had stopped over for a meal some months previously.

Cap decided it was best to leave the sheriff and his own men to continue the scout, while he started the long, cold ride back to Clifton alone. He pulled in around eleven that Saturday night and he figured that either on foot or horseback he'd covered a good hundred miles.

He dropped his guns and gear behind the bar of a saloon and hit it across the street to a barber-shop. One barber was just leaving and the second man was finishing off the last customer.

"I'd like a hot bath," Cap said a little bluntly.

"We're closed," the barber barked. "God Almighty! Don't you think we ever rest?"

"I'll take care of it by myself. I'm tired and dirty and sore, and I need a bath." Without further ado Cap walked straight down the hall to a bathroom and turned on the water.

The partition ran only part way to the ceiling, and Cap could hear the barber sounding off. "By God, that sonofabitch is taking charge. I'll see who owns this shop!"

When Cap heard him stomping down the hall toward the tiny bath room, he filled a tin cup full of hot water. The barber pushed open the door and Cap let him have it.

Angry and half-scalded he ran through his shop and into the street. Cap could hear him calling to the town marshal: "I got a goddam crazy man in there! I want you to arrest him!"

Cap knew the peace officer, and he could hear him coming on down the hall and then fumbling with the knob of the bathroom door.

"Say, feller! Wacha think you're a-doin'?" the marshal demanded gruffly.

"Well, right now I'm climbing a tree," Cap answered. "What in hell do you think I'm doing?"

"I'm comin' in and find out."

Cap grabbed his faithful tin cup and filled it. Cautiously the marshal turned the handle and peeked in, his pistol in his right hand. When he saw who it was he broke out a laugh and closed the door.

He was still laughing when he went out into the street. "Hell! That's Cap Mossman," he explained between chuckles. "You better leave him alone."

The barber dutifully waited while Cap soaked out the stiff joints and the dull aches. When he'd put on fresh clothes, Cap strolled out through the shop, leaving a silver dollar on the marble stand under the mirror.

He found the town marshal across the street in the bar and bought him a pair of drinks. Most of the time Cap was still taking cigars for himself.

-- 7 --

Cap seemed to find a deep satisfaction in riding lone missions. "Little Black John" Slaughter might have had something to do with that.

Slaughter was a slender, under-sized Texan, with a pair of piercing black eyes, who'd come into the border country in the early Seventies. He'd fought Apaches and Mexicans, Texans and bad men of all kinds, and he'd never been scratched.

When Tombstone, county seat of Cochise County, was out of hand, the better element elected John sheriff and, almost single-handed, he'd gone a long ways toward cleaning it up. This was back in the early Nineties, and oddly enough, a boy named Burt Alvord, who later got running with the wild bunch, was John's deputy.

Slaughter had a way of riding off by himself, his double-barreled shotgun resting across his saddle in front of him. A day or two later he'd come back to Tombstone leading a horse packing an empty saddle. They told the tale that once John killed a man he was after while the outlaw was asleep: John was just too kind-hearted to awaken him, so the story went.

It is not improbable that Slaughter's technique and efficiency were sources of considerable inspiration to Cap and his Rangers. The sheriff never bragged about his lonely journeys and his quiet triumphs. Cap was much the same, but certainly Mossman took no pride or joy in the sheer business of killing men. And he found the reputation he was gaining was not entirely to his liking.

He much preferred to let his men carry on the high drama and get the credit; but now and again he was confronted with a nasty job he could not very well relegate to anyone else. On these rare occasions he did not hesitate to follow through.

He had a number of friends among the better class of Mexican-Americans in Tucson, and one of them had a daughter who was a little on the gay side. At a dance she had met a dashing young *caballero* from Sonora, who seemed well supplied with gold dollars and a rather appealing spirit of bravado and recklessness.

Later they secretly met and he urged her to be his girl. After he betrayed her she sobbed out her remorse to him, and he feared she might tell her parents. In an outbreak of anger he lost his head and cut her throat. When her body was found a day later, he had disappeared.

Cap contacted his secret sources of information, and soon found out the murderer's name and that he lived in the little Mexican city of Altar, some twenty miles due south of the border town of Sasabe. The boy was of a prominent family and Cap felt it might be embarrassing to call on Colonel Kosterlitzky for help.

He promptly assigned the dirty job to himself. Dead men tell no tales, and he who travels alone travels fastest. Then, too, he felt that since he knew the girl personally and was a friend of the family, he had a special responsibility.

It was sixty miles to Sasabe, and darkness had closed in when he quietly rode up to the house of an acquaintance connected with the U. S. Customs. He asked to be put up, and added that he preferred that his visit be kept a secret.

Early the following night he tied his horse in a clump of bush back of a house on the outskirts of Altar. He had no plans but he did have an objective. Off toward the center of the town he could hear music, and since it was Saturday he surmised there was a *baile* going on. He was sure his man would be there.

Cap was wearing a broad-brimmed border hat, and wind and sun had given him such a rich brown tan that in the dim light he could pass as a Mexican ranchero. Quietly he made his way to the alley in the rear of the dance-hall. It was dark here and even the street in front was poorly lit.

Slowly he worked his way along a side wall toward the street. A barefoot Mexican boy was loitering at the corner of the building. Cap whistled softly and motioned for him to step toward him.

In perfect Spanish he told the boy to look in the hall for the Mexican he named, and tell him that a gentleman outside had something for him. He gave the boy a silver peso and explained that he was to say nothing to anyone, nor was he to offer any more information to the Mexican. Cap would be here along the side wall of the hall waiting for his friend to come.

He slipped into the deep shadows, seventy or eighty feet back from the dimly lit street. After several minutes of waiting he could see the figure of a jaunty, well-built young Mexican coming alone toward him. There was no one else in sight.

"Yo estoy aquí, amigo," (I am here, friend) Cap said in pleasant Spanish.

"Who is it?" the man asked in his native tongue. "What have you for me?"

It was the 14-inch blade of a Bowie knife that Cap had. He made one more quick slash, wiped the blade on the fallen man's white shirt, and then slipped away. There had been no outcry or sound of struggle.

Within ten minutes he was riding northward through the

outskirts at an easy trot that would arouse no suspicion. When he had passed beyond the town he let out his mount. The best horse in Mexico could not have overtaken him. In an oddly gruesome way he was happy; he had indulged himself in a bit of poetic if bloody justice.

It wasn't quite midnight when he reached the border at Sasabe. His friend had arranged for his entrance without formality. At daylight he was pounding the road to Tucson.

That little episode, too, has been kept a close secret for fifty years.

-- 8 --

Augustin Chacon had killed no Americans since Cap Mossman had organized the Rangers—but he had killed plenty before that time. His record ran somewhere between ten and twenty-nine.

But it was not only the number he had murdered but the downright cruelty and inhumanity of the man that had given him his sinister reputation. At times he seemed to kill purely for the sadistic joy of seeing men in their death agonies.

He was tall and powerful, with long arms and great hands, and unquestionably he had considerable Indian blood. Within the last year or two he had grown a bushy beard that had won him the nickname of *Paludo,* or Hairy One.

In one sweep across the border, a few months before the Rangers came into being, Chacon and his gang had held up a gambling house in Jerome, killed two prospector-hunters, raided a sheep camp up toward Phoenix and murdered two sheep shearers, and then robbed a stage-coach enroute to Agua Fría. For two weeks he played hide-and-go-seek with sheriffs' posses, finally slipping across the border to the safety of his hide-out in the Sierre Madras mountains of Sonora. That one adventure brought him several packmule-loads of loot and a record of four Americans dead.

It was only one of several raids he was credited with making on the mining camps and lonely settlements of the Territory. It was almost as if the spirit of the Apache Cochise or Mangas Coloradas, or old Geronimo himself, had settled in his lean, hard body. But Chacon completely lacked the elements of greatness and obscured justice that marked these Indian leaders as something far more than mere killers. He had copied only their stealth and cruelty.

Apparently there was little or none of the typical Robin Hood about him. He was *puro bandido*. Yet he did have a certain way with women, and the feeling among the poorer Spanish-speaking elements of Arizona was by no means entirely against him. To certain eyes he was the abused and the hunted, who struck back only in self-defense against the dominant race that ran the courts and "the law," and had cornered most of the wealth.

The legend of the man eventually far outgrew his true stature. He was credited with most of the unsolved crimes of his day, and as time went on his very name struck cold terror into the hearts of men who lived or traveled the distant trails and isolated areas. The most generous thing that could be said in his favor was that he did not molest women; American men were his game.

Almost five years before the formation of the Rangers Chacon had robbed a store near Morenci in the Clifton country, and in a diabolical surge of hate he had hacked to pieces the body of the owner, Becker, and then looted his place. The sheriff of Graham County immediately organized a posse and trailed the outlaws. They caught up with them in a box canyon and apparently had them surrounded.

A deputy-sheriff named Pablo Salcido explained to the sheriff that he was sure they had treed Chacon's gang, and since he and

Chacon had once been friends he thought he might get him to surrender. He was told to try it if he wished, but to take no unnecessary chances.

The deputy tied a white handkerchief to his rifle barrel and stepped out into the open. He shouted that he was Pablo Salcido, and he asked Chacon, as an old friend, to let him talk to him.

"Come on down here if you want to see me," Chacon yelled from his side of the canyon.

The deputy boldly walked toward the spot, and when hardly more than fifty feet away, Chacon suddenly rose to his feet and killed his one-time friend. The posse closed in at this betrayal, and shot Chacon through the arm and the lungs. That night most of the outlaws managed to escape but the leader was found at dawn more dead than alive. His tough body pulled him through and he was brought to Solomonville for trial, quickly convicted of murdering Becker and sentenced to be hanged.

He had many active sympathizers among the Mexicans in neighboring mining camps, and one of them was a young woman who apparenly was his *querida.* No sweetheart could have been more loyal.

Knowing how desperate his prisoner was, the sheriff assigned a special death-watch guard, and everything sent in to him was carefully examined. Nevertheless, the girl was able to hide a thin hacksaw blade in the heavy binding of a Bible, and get it to his cell.

Her next move was of a slightly more delicate nature. She pretended to the night guard that while she had once been interested in Chacon, now she was smitten with the officer himself. She was a warm and pretty thing, with large, wide-set black eyes and a soft voice. It was gentle caresses that she wanted, and this Americano was big and handsome. She played her part so well that one night when the date of Chacon's execution was less than a week off, she teased the guard into taking her into the jailer's office. They could hear the inmates singing, while two of the prisoners made music on a guitar and concertina. It was pleasant to make love to this strange musical accompaniment. Certainly the sound of Chacon's hacksaw did not reach their ears.

The next night the girl returned, and this time the guard offered no resistance to her charms. He had never realized before that he was such a great lover.

The scaffold was finished two days later. In less than twenty-four hours Chacon would be marched out and hanged by the neck until he was dead. The guard was thinking of this very fact when he returned to his duties at midnight from his tryst with the warm little Mexican girl. She had held to him for a long time this night. And the singing in the cells had been unusually lusty.

He unlocked the outer door of the jail block and sauntered back to Chacon's cell. My God! It was empty!

He found his key and opened the steel door. Three bars of the outside window had been neatly sawed in two. The captive bird had flown.

He raced to the courtyard and found a rope dangling over the wall. He'd have plenty to explain to the sheriff.

During the next three or four years Chacon was on the loose, depredating pretty much where and how he chose. As far as Arizona was concerned, he was definitely Public Enemy Number One.

When the Governor and his friends had brought pressure on Mossman to organize the Rangers, it was understood that at the top of his list of arch-criminals to be checked off stood the gaunt, bearded figure of Chacon. It was a point of honor that Cap must get him.

As the rumors of Mossman's prowess turned into legends there was considerable good-natured banter on all sides as to why he did not kill or capture the bandit. Cap's enemies, and even the peace officers who were envious of his reputation, dropped sly hints concerning his failure.

More and more criticism of the high-handed methods of the Rangers began to drift to Governor Murphy, and he found out that he could touch Cap's one sore spot by the slightest reference to the outlaw. The Governor felt that often the Captain was holding back details of his cleaning-up operations, and at times there was a little sting in his good-natured banter. "If you're so good why don't you get me Chacon?" he would needle Cap.

Mossman would grin and tell him to give him something easy to do, but the implications stuck in his craw. His mutual arrangement with Colonel Kosterlitzky of the Sonora Rurales did not include the right to ask that friendly official to help him run down Chacon. After all, the bandit was a Mexican citizen. The privilege of permitting either Mexican or Arizona officials to cross the border was limited to the pursuit of their own nationals: Americans chasing Americans, and Mexicans chasing Mexicans. Certainly Arizona officers could not legally cross into Mexico to kill or capture Mexican citizens.

Mossman, with Chacon sticking in his mind like a cockleburr, made it clear to his underworld contacts that if any of them put him on the trail of the bandit, he would be rewarded handsomely out of Cap's own pocket. And he often talked with his important friends over ways and means of reaching Chacon.

Judge Barnes had long been Federal District Judge, and despite the fact that he was entirely on the opposite side of the fence he had gained the respect and confidence of a man named Burt Alvord, who had grown up around Tombstone in its tough and prosperous days. Alvord was a powerfully built, dark-complexioned man, with a bald head and a killer's eye. It was said that he was half-Texan and half-Indian, which certainly was no gentle combination.

At one time he had worked as a cowboy for John Slaughter, and when "Little Black John" was sheriff he had on various occasions used Alvord as one of his deputies. Alvord had been working with Slaughter when John had had his famous run-in with Chacon.

The Mexican had boasted that he'd like to swap lead with the American sheriff. John was more than willing—as long as he had his double-barreled shotgun, loaded with buckshot, along. He didn't need Alvord to help him, but the deputy stuck pretty close.

The night came when Slaughter was tipped off just where the famous bandit could be located. He went after him alone.

Chacon was flushed back of a house of easy virtue, and it seemed sure that Slaughter finally had him. The Mexican, taken off-base, ran for his life. That split second when Old John raised his gun and fired, Chacon tripped over a wire and rolled down a slope. The buckshot whistled over his head, and he escaped in the darkness.

From his job of deputy-sheriff Burt Alvord slipped into various dubious occupations, including cattle rustling, horse stealing and plain and fancy gun fighting. He was as hard to catch as the Irishman's flea. At one moment he would be on the side of the law, and the next moment against it. He rode shotgun for gold deliveries and did odd jobs for Wells, Fargo and so knew the exact trains that carried heavy shipments of cash. It was this last unique bit of knowledge that was his undoing.

Along with a killer named Bob Downing, who had been one of the Sam Bass gang of Texas outlaws, and a slippery-eel named Billy Stiles, he planned the robbery of an express car at Cochise Junction, a few miles west of Willcox. At this time Alvord was town marshal of Willcox, and Downing was his undercover man. Billy Stiles, a small, dark man, with a large touch of Mexican blood, served as his special deputy.

Billy Stiles and an outlaw named Matt Burts are supposed to to have been picked to do the actual train hold-up job. Getting the drop on the express messenger, they compelled the engineer to cut loose the engine and express car, and run them a mile down the track. Then they blew open the safe, and collected what was reputed to be $80,000 in gold coin. They quickly filled their saddlebags, and rode their unshod horses across the hard, dry bed of a lake, galloped east and hurried to the adobe house at the edge of Willcox where Alvord lived alone. Turning over all but a few of the gold coins to him, they quietly headed for town and established their alibis.

It was the drunken bragging and the ringing of golden tens and twenties on the saloon bars by Bob Downing, that gave away the perfect crime. The three were arrested and Billy Stiles was trapped into confessing, but at the last moment he drew back from signing the document and it was worthless. He and Downing and Burts had received only a few hundred dollars each from Alvord out of the great haul.

It was all a mixed-up business, with the Wells, Fargo and railroad detectives interested primarily in getting back the stolen cash rather than in convictions. They still felt they could use Stiles in finding the cache and they let him loose. He called at the jail in Tombstone and Jailer Bravin refused his request to see Alvord. In the argument Billy pulled a gun, shot Bravin in the leg, secured the cell keys and releasing his partner led the way south into Sonora. Alvord alone knew where the gold loot was buried, while the slippery Stiles was still only his tool.

It is at this point that Alvord ties into the story of Chacon, a desperado no tougher than the American save in pure brutality. Billy Stiles did not rate as the equal of either in cruelty, intelligence or desperation. He was on the borderline of being a weakling, even though he was remarkably fast with a gun.

It was only natural that sooner or later the two master crooks,

Chacon and Alvord, should become friends. "The law" was against them both. Each was a hunted man, and each had to live by his wits and his skill on the draw.

Cap Mossman had several times talked over the Chacon problem with Judge Barnes, and finally the Judge had said: "Cap, your best bet is to try and contact Burt Alvord. It's a ticklish job, and you might never come back."

Cap agreed. He knew all about Alvord, although he had never seen him. The bank robber, incidentally, was high on his Rangers' list of musts.

The Judge explained that he had a hunch that Alvord was ready to come in. He had a gunshot wound in his right wrist that had never healed and that pained him considerably. Cap might make a deal that the Judge and the Governor would help get Alvord off with a light sentence, if he'd take Cap to Chacon and then come in and surrender.

"Where'll I find Alvord, Judge?" Cap asked.

"I don't know, but anytime you figure you can locate him in his hide-out in Sonora I'll give you a letter to him."

Mossman was getting somewhere now and he was grateful for the help.

"I'd also suggest you contact Alvord's wife in Willcox," the Judge added. "You can tell her that I sent you to her."

It was early in April and Mossman dropped everything else. He found Alvord's wife discouraged and living almost in poverty. She could not tell him much about her husband, but she agreed with Judge Barnes that it was best for him to give up and let his friends try to get him off as lightly as they could.

Cap quietly went on with his search for Alvord's hide-out. Finally he got a tip that Billy Stiles had a half-brother working as a pump operator for an English smelter at Minas Prietas, on a branch line far down on the Nogales-Guaymas railroad in lower

Sonora. He'd be sure to know Alvord, so Cap hurriedly got in touch with Judge Barnes and asked for the letter.

The Judge wrote it out in longhand and it was straightforward and clear; most of the witnesses against Alvord were either in jail or were dead, or had left the country. His chances of acquittal, or at the worst a light sentence, were good. If he'd help Cap Mossman and then come in and give himself up, the Judge would defend him for nothing. He closed with the word that Alvord's wife was lonely and in desperate circumstances, and that she was being urged to get a divorce. He, the Judge, had advised her to await developments.

"You understand the chances you're taking, don't you, Cap?" the Judge asked. "Don't forget, this Alvord is a hard man and a killer. I certainly wish you good luck."

Mossman slipped down to Nogales and quietly boarded the train south a few moments before it pulled out. Two or three of his friends cautioned him his timing was wrong; both Sheriff Dell Lewis, of Cochise County, and Tom Turner, of Santa Cruz County, had made secret expeditions into Sonora in search of Alvord—and failed. The outlaw was stirred up and resentful. One false move and Cap's life wouldn't be worth a *copita* of mescal.

At Tores he took the branch line to Minas Prietas, and went straight to the English manager of the smelter with his story; but the official advised Cap against the venture. If he still insisted, he'd furnish him with a four-mule outfit that would take him the twenty-four miles back in the hills where Stiles' half-brother was running the big steam pump that drove the water up to the smelter. But he felt that the risks were too great.

Mossman was still determined on taking the long chance and early the following morning he started out with a driver. He found Stiles' half-brother skeptical and hard-boiled, but Cap talked fast and finally showed him Judge Barnes' letter to Alvord.

The pump operator, now convinced that Cap would do Alvord no harm, fixed him up with a horse and a Mexican saddle, and at daybreak gave him explicit directions as to how to reach Alvord's hide-out.

Mossman's years of following trails and his sixth sense of direction stood him in good stead. It was late in the afternoon when he rounded a sharp shoulder of a hill and there, on a slope not more than two hundred yards away, he saw a big man standing in front of a stone hut, a rifle held in the crook of his left arm.

Cap kept straight on, his hands obviously free and no weapon showing. When he was not more than twenty feet away he pulled up. He knew from the pictures he had studied that he was face to face with the outlaw.

"I presume I am addressing Burt Alvord?" he said in a casual tone.

"Who are you?" the man snapped back.

"I'm Captain Mossman of the Arizona Rangers."

"The hell you are! Where's your gang?"

"Mr. Alvord, I'm one of those poor devils who travels alone."

"You haven't anyone with you?"

"No, not a soul. But I have got a letter from your friend Judge Barnes, and news about your wife."

Cap could see the muzzles of three or four rifle barrels poking out of slits in the stone wall, and all leveled at him.

"Mind telling those boys of yours to point their guns in some other direction?" he asked with a smile. "I have no weapon except the pistol that I always carry. You can see I'm helpless."

Alvord shouted an order in Spanish. Then he turned to Mossman. "Get down and let's have the letter."

Alvord took the note and slowly spelled out the words. When

he'd finished he turned to Mossman and asked him what he wanted.

"I'll tell you when we get a chance to talk alone. But first I'd like to get something to eat."

Alvord led him down the trail to a Mexican sheep herder's camp, and they ate beans and mutton and *tortillas*. Then several bottles of mescal were produced, and the men sat around and drank the fiery alcohol straight. One of them admired the silver-and gold-inlaid single-action Colt that had been presented to Cap by some friends. He asked to see it.

Mossman demanded to be handed his gun in turn, and they exchanged weapons. The Mexican, a little drunk and mean, remarked how nice it would be to keep Cap's beautiful gun so he might show it to his girl. Cap smiled and remarked in his faultless Spanish: "But think how sad it would be if someone showed her your dead body."

The Mexican jumped to his feet, but Alvord ordered his gang to quiet down. "This man is my guest," he shouted. "Give him back his gun, *tu,* and let him alone!"

That night when they got back to the stone cabin, Cap and Alvord sat apart from the others. Alvord showed him his bandaged wrist. He explained how it would not heal and that it bothered him constantly.

Cap examined it and said it would have to be amputated if Alvord didn't soon get to a doctor.

"What do you want out of me?" Alvord finally questioned.

"Put me in touch with Chacon somewhere near the border," Cap answered bluntly. "I'll help you get acquitted if you give yourself up after I get Chacon and I'll split all the rewards for Chacon equally between you and Billy Stiles."

Alvord reviewed the possibilities. He knew the bandit but he vowed he was suspicious and wily and would kill at the drop

of the hat. But maybe he could bring in Mossman as a member
of a new gang Alvord could pretend he was organizing.

Cap explained that Colonel Greene's finest race horses were
only a few miles above the border on the Arizona side. Alvord
should suggest to Chacon that he had a friend who'd just broken
jail who knew all about the thoroughbreds and exactly how they
could be rounded up and driven off.

Alvord had one more stipulation: Mossman must get Billy
Stiles to act as a go-between. Neither of them fully trusted him,
but he was the best they had for the job. Cap agreed. He'd put
Stiles on the payroll of the Rangers, although he knew he would
get hell for doing it.

Mossman started back early the following morning. He found
things were starting to move rapidly at home. President Teddy
Roosevelt had just appointed Major Brodie, of the Rough Riders,
as Territorial Governor. And—as Mossman was to say a thousand times—"the devastating blight of the Rough Riders was for
the next seven years to spread over the Southwest."

Cap duly submitted his resignation to Governor Brodie. His
one concern was that he would have to leave the Rangers before
he had finished with Chacon. Cap had quietly appointed Stiles
as a Ranger and assigned him to the border, and warned him of
the secrecy of his mission. Mossman had hoped for immediate
results but the Mexican gods-of-the-chaparral grind exceedingly
slow. Weeks slipped by and no word came from Alvord. Time
was running out for the captain of the Rangers.

In desperation he got in touch with United States Marshal
W. H. McCord at Phoenix, and asked to be appointed a Deputy
United States Marshal, so that ostensibly he could have more
freedom of movement outside the boundaries of Arizona. McCord
agreed and Cap's commission was dated July 2, 1902.

Mossman felt a little easier now. Governor Brodie sent him a most gracious letter, and asked him to stay on as Captain of Rangers until he could choose a proper replacement. This gave Cap more precious time, but he now had his position as a Deputy U. S. Marshal to fall back on.

The capture of Chacon had become little short of an obsession with him. He had vowed to get him and he was going to keep right on trying no matter the odds against him. His pride, his stubbornness, his considerable ego, were all involved. He was more than willing to bet his life on even the thinnest chance of success. But he was helpless to do anything on his own.

All his hopes lay in the hands of two completely unreliable and vicious men. He had won Billy Stiles with a promise that half the reward still offered by Graham County for Chacon's capture, would go to him. It was not the other half of the money that interested Alvord; it was the opportunity to get his wrist healed, to return to his wife, and someday to dig up the gold loot from the Cochise train robbery that still lay buried in a spot known only to himself.

But even these two confederates could at best help only up to a certain point. Alvord might not be able to lure Chacon near the border, no matter how honestly he tried.

Mossman saw clearly that even if he was finally taken to Chacon as a confederate, there was no assurance that the bandit might not be suspicious and try to kill him. That would not be an easy matter against a man as fast and deadly as Cap. He might still be able to get in the first shot.

But he didn't want to do that. He wanted to bring Chacon back alive. Otherwise, his enemies and the skeptics might say that it was all talk; that he hadn't really killed the great *bandido,* but only some poor *pelado* whom he'd got the drop on.

Precious days were slipping by. And then new trouble came roaring in for Cap from an entirely unexpected quarter.

On August 19th the Los Angeles *Times* printed a long dispatch from Bisbee telling of an alleged fight that three Rangers, including Captain Mossman, had had with two Bisbee policemen. Two Rangers were arrested, so the story went, and were thrown into jail. Later a Ranger secured a key at the point of a gun and released the Rangers. It was largely a pack of lies and exaggerations but it proved the temper of the moment. There had been a little trouble and two of his Rangers had been taken to the local jail, but Mossman had them immediately released.

A drunken hanger-on, who a short time before had been arrested for wife-beating, was hired by a dive keeper to circulate a petition among the town's riff-raff, calling on the Governor to relieve Mossman at once. In answer every merchant and respectable business man in town signed another petition that read:

"We, the undersigned citizens and taxpayers of Bisbee, Cochise County, Territory of Arizona, regardless of party affiliation, being aware of the stigma attempted to be cast on the character and efficiency of Burton C. Mossman, Captain of the Arizona Rangers, do hereby attest and proclaim our entire belief, confidence and knowledge in his character as a gentleman, efficiency as an officer of the law and uprightness as a citizen and also having at heart and appreciating the invaluable services of the Rangers, one and all, in protecting our interests and property against any violation of the law, we do hereby extend our thanks to and express our recognition of the valiant efforts and faithful services of this organization while under the command of Captain Burton C. Mossman."

Among the eighty-nine signatures were those of the Rev. H. M. Shields and the Rev. J. G. Pritchard.

Mossman was on duty in Bowie at the moment and when he heard of the turn of affairs he wrote a letter to Governor Brodie. At the same time he sent the following wire to W. A. Nash, at Bisbee:

"My resignation was tendered Governor Brodie in July will be accepted August 31."

And still there was no word from Billy Stiles and Alvord.

September 1st came on a Monday and, true to form, a former Rough Rider became the new Captain of the Arizona Rangers. Tom Rynning, considerably lacking in Mossman's intelligence and finesse, had once been a sergeant in the famous old Sixth Cavalry, and had served in the short and romantic Spanish-American war as a Lieutenant in Troop B.

Cap still had his commission as a Deputy United States Marshal. He had run out of time as a Ranger, but he wasn't giving up hope.

The lamps in Bisbee's streets were just being lit the next evening when he received the message he had so long waited for. The following day he was to have a rendezvous with Chacon.

It barely entered his head that it might be a rendezvous with death.

-- 9 --

Billy Stiles brought him the news from Alvord, and within an hour the two started at an easy trot for the border at Naco.

He was to join Alvord and Chacon on below with a plan to gather up Colonel Greene's horses. Cap and Stiles crossed into the Mexican town and then quietly walked their mounts down the dirt street that led toward the outskirts.

It was daybreak when they pulled in at Carizzo Springs, a good twenty-five miles on below. They were both worried when there was no sight of Chacon and Alvord. Something had failed to click.

They lay hidden in the chaparral most of the day, but in late afternoon rode north toward the border, hoping to contact the pair. Cap had by no means been sure of Stiles' loyalty, but the temporary Ranger seemed so distressed at the way the plans had miscarried that Mossman began to feel sure Billy would stick with him. In a gesture that showed how worn out he was, Cap leaned over and put his hand on the back of Billy's saddle, as their horses walked side by side up a slope.

Billy had his coat tied behind the cantle and as Cap's hand fell on the soft roll his fingers unmistakably felt a pair of old-fashioned handcuffs that Billy had sewed into the bottom of the lining. Mossman made no comment but his suspicions were now aroused. Stiles had said nothing about carrying the cuffs, and it was a bad turn of affairs for Cap.

They were riding along the east slope of the San José Mountains just below Naco, when they spotted two figures on horseback coming toward them. It was shortly after nine, and the night was fairly dark.

Alvord made no attempt at a formal introduction. He acknowledged Mossman as *amigo,* and Cap and Chacon nodded toward each other and both uttered the simple greeting *buenas noches* (good-evening). Mossman could feel the back of his hair rise like the hackle on a fighting dog when he encounters a strange animal.

He watched the Mexican looking him over in the dim light. Suddenly he realized that he had been wrong in riding his best horse, with his concho-mounted saddle and fine gear. His clothes and his whole outfit were hardly those of a man who had only recently broken jail and was on the hoot-owl trail.

Cap started talking about Colonel Greene's fine horses. Even his famous stallion was turned out in pasture, along with a bunch of thoroughbred mares. The four men could swoop up the whole herd and drive them deep down into Sonora.

Chacon made no contribution except to grunt that it was too dark to attempt the raid this night. Cap agreed they had better camp out the rest of the night and then start the next day. They could cut the international fence a few miles on west of Naco and he'd lead them straight to the horses.

They pulled back off the trail into the mesquite and greasewood. Stiles hustled a fire, and the men laid out their saddle blankets and propped themselves against tree trunks. Each man carried a pistol and a Winchester, and Cap could see a sheathed knife on Chacon's left hip.

It was the night of September 3rd, and here in this high country there was already a chill in the air.

"Billy, how about riding to Naco and bringing back a bottle of whiskey?" Cap suggested.

Chacon made no comment but Alvord figured it was a good idea. The Mexican seemed to turn morose, and his roving black eyes missed nothing. He was obviously not quite sure of things.

It started raining before Stiles returned, and Cap put on his yellow slicker. He managed to slip his pistol out of its holster, and as he sat huddled against a tree his right hand gripped the butt of the gun lying across his leg under his long coat. He wondered if he could live the night out.

Chacon refused a drink, and after Billy and Alvord had gulped down big slugs, Mossman took several nips so that he would keep awake and alert. He could trust neither of his two confederates, and he began to feel that at any moment Chacon might try to kill him.

At daybreak Burt Alvord caught up his horse and without an explanation threw on the saddle.

"*Adonde va, Alberto?*" (Where are you going?) Chacon questioned.

"Where I can get some good water, Augustine," Alvord answered.

Cap walked over close to him and out of the corner of his mouth Alvord whispered, "Watch Stiles." That was all.

Mossman was on double guard now. It was evident that Alvord had cleared out for good. He had fulfilled his part of the contract; he had put Mossman in touch with Chacon, and close to the border to boot.

Stiles rekindled the fire and produced a chunk of bacon and cold biscuit. Cap watched as the two fried thick slices of the bacon on the sharp ends of mesquite sticks. He pretended that he didn't want any breakfast.

The play was swiftly reaching the moment of decision, as Cap's mind ran through the various possibilities that presented themselves. He was sure that Chacon was now wise to him, while Alvord's tip not to trust Stiles had fully confirmed his suspicions first aroused when he had discovered the hidden handcuffs.

The two men at the fire lit loosely rolled, fragrant Mexican cigarettes. Cap walked straight up to Chacon and asked him for one. Chacon, squatting on his heels, handed up the pack. Without lifting his eyes Cap picked out a cigarette and returned the pack to Chacon. Then he stepped back.

Slowly he unrolled the paper and carefully rolled it tighter. Then he reached down with his left hand and picked up a glowing brand of mesquite, his eyes never leaving Chacon. After lighting his cigarette, and with Chacon's black eyes watching every move, he passed the brand to his right hand.

As he dropped it to the fire his right hand whipped out his pistol. "Hands up!" he shouted, throwing down on Chacon.

Deliberately, and with tantalizing slowness, the bandit raised his hands.

"Disarm him, Billy!" Cap ordered. "Throw his gun and belt behind him."

For an instant he swung his cocked pistol at his confederate. "Now slip on the handcuffs."

"What handcuffs?" Billy demanded.

"The ones sewed in your coat—you double-crossing rat!"

Billy made no comment as he ripped open the lining and took out the cuffs. Slowly he put them on the Mexican.

Cap backed off to where his rifle was leaning against a tree. Without moving his eyes he picked up the gun with his left hand, and still holding to his pistol, pulled down the loading lever and threw in a shell. He now held a loaded and cocked Winchester that was twice as effective as a pistol.

"Billy," he ordered sharply, "unbuckle your own gun and drop it behind you."

Billy started to argue but Cap swung the rifle toward him. Then he moved behind the two men, and with the toe of his boot pulled the two pistols well to the rear. Cap made no effort to retrieve either the pistols or the two Winchesters.

"Catch the horses and saddle them, Billy," he ordered. "I'll kill you the first wrong move you make."

Billy Stiles led off the little procession, holding the rope that was around the neck of Chacon's horse. The Mexican rode in the middle, his handcuffed hands in front of him. His horse was bridled and he could manage to touch the reins.

Cap returned his rifle to its boot, and his six-shooter was lightly holstered. He was confident he was master and he took down his rope and made a small loop. It was no mean weapon in itself.

His chief worry was to keep out of sight of any passing troop of Rurales that might be riding out of Naco. There had been a big detail of them camped near there the night before and if they happened by within the next half-hour or so, they might catch sight of the three men and ride in to investigate.

Cap decided he'd never let them take Chacon from him. If he was caught, he'd kill the bandit and then ride hell-bent for the border. But he wanted to bring in Chacon alive.

They kept off the main road and then cut west across rolling country. On below them to the north they could see the winding snake that was the border fence. That was Cap's goal.

Now and again he could see Chacon pulling back on his reins. The hondo of Cap's rope would crack down on the rump of the bandit's horse and he would shout at Chacon to keep going. Finally he slipped the bridle off Chacon's horse and hung it on his own saddle horn. Stiles, riding ahead, could lead him better now with his rope.

They were less than a mile from the fence when Cap saw Chacon's hands gripping the great round pommel of his Mexican saddle. Apparently he was about to make one last desperate attempt to escape. Cap built a small loop and dropped it over the bandit's head.

"Take your hands off your saddle!" Cap barked at him. "You're going across the border with me if I have to half-sole you and drag you across."

They pulled up at the heavy wire fence and with his pistol in his right hand Mossman reached into a saddle pocket with his left and brought out a pair of heavy wire cutters. He threw them at Stiles' feet and told him to cut the fence. They were five or six miles west of Naco.

On ahead lay the railway line that curved down in a great half-circle from Bisbee and then headed north for its junction with the main Southern Pacific line at Benson. A mile up from the border was a switch and siding called Packard, after one of Colonel Greene's old partners.

The three men had barely passed through the hole in the border fence when Cap caught a glimpse of smoke rising from a train moving south from Bisbee. Before long he could hear the rattle and bang of the little train as it pounded across the desert.

He shouted for Stiles to go faster. When they had waited at the line for Stiles to cut the wire, he had taken the rope off Chacon's neck; he wanted no one to think he was afraid of the bandit. He had hung the rope around his saddle horn and he now slipped it off and swung free the hondo. It was an ideal persuader for Chacon's horse to keep up.

He could now actually see the train rolling along through the mesquite like a drunken man. Stiles seemed to catch the drama, and he put his horse into a gallop.

Somehow everything was working out according to the schedule that Cap unconsciously had laid out. He had only to reach the tracks in time to flag the train. He knew what to do from then on.

The engine was not more than three hundred yards away when Cap slipped down from his horse and waved his hat. The old coal-burner ground to a stop. The conductor came running down the side of the train from the middle coach to see what the trouble was. He had no gold shipment, but it was an ideal place for a hold-up.

"Take the horses back to Bisbee and keep your mouth shut,"

Cap ordered Stiles. With his pistol stuck in Chacon's belly he helped him down from his saddle.

The conductor recognized Cap, and his fears evaporated quickly. Mossman marched Chacon up the steps and into the smoking car. He prodded him to the front seat, and sat directly behind him.

The delay made the local a little late at Benson, and the through train was waiting for it. On the depot platform almost directly in front of where the smoking car stopped, stood Jim Parks, sheriff of Graham County. Of all the men in the world that Cap would have chosen to meet him at this particular moment, "Hard Times" Parks would have been his first choice.

Before he even saw Mossman, Parks recognized the hand-cuffed Chacon shuffling down the car steps. It was hard for him to believe his eyes.

"How are you, Chacon?" he blurted out in Spanish. "What happens?"

"Buenos días, Don Jamie," (Good-morning, Mr. Jim,) Chacon answered, a grin showing through his black beard.

Then the sheriff saw Mossman. After a swift greeting Parks asked if he could be of any help.

"Yes, Jim; if you've got some leg irons and a good pair of handcuffs," Cap answered. "I'm officially turning him over to you right now, Jim. He's all yours."

It was five years since Chacon had escaped from the Solomon-ville jail, the night before he was to be hanged. Mossman's idea had been that he would personally deliver him at Solomonville to Parks. But the sheriff had by a happy chance met him here at Benson on his way back from taking prisoners to the Yuma penitentiary.

Chacon was hustled into the depot, and the waiting-room cleaned out. Parks brought out his leg irons, but so alive still was the fame of the killer that the sheriff handed his gun to Cap before he reached down to put the irons on the tall prisoner. And he was careful to fasten the shiny new handcuffs over Chacon's wrists before he unlocked the old ones.

The conductor of the through train gave the peace officers all the time they wanted. Chacon made no comment nor asked any favors.

When he was arraigned before the judge at Solomonville as an escaped criminal under sentence of death, he was asked to stand up and face the court.

"Are you Augustin Chacon?" the judge demanded.

"I am Augustin Chacon," he answered proudly and defiantly. "And I am not afraid to die."

On November 23rd, a little more than two and a half months after Mossman brought him across the border, he stepped to the trap door on the scaffold, and Sheriff Jim Parks asked him if he had any final word to say.

He turned and looked Parks straight in the eye. There was no tremor in his voice or hand.

"*Adiós amigo!*" he said. Then his eyes turned to roam over the crowd in the jail yard below.

Cap Mossman was with Colonel Bill Greene in the old Waldorf in New York City that day. He had ridden the accommodation train back to Bisbee on the morning he had turned to Chacon over to Jim Parks. His job was finished. He had done the impossible; he had brought out Chacon alive. But in doing so he had kidnaped a Mexican citizen—and there might be serious international complications.

Cap knew that Colonel Greene was in New York, and he had had a dozen cordial invitations to visit him there. Greene was sure they could work out some big deal together. Now might be an ideal time for Cap to try his luck. And it would certainly be smart for him to make himself hard to find until Chacon was hanged. Billy Stiles was the only other witness to the kidnaping and no court in Arizona would take his word on oath.

Cap had $30,000 in the bank in Bisbee, and he drew a thousand in cash and had his balance transferred to Thatcher's First National Bank in Pueblo, Colorado. The Thatcher brothers were old friends and his employers in the Bloody Basin days. While he was at it, he figured he had better cut all contacts with Arizona.

A great open world lay ahead of him. He reached out for it and for the bright, gay life that it promised.

It would be difficult to replace the excitement and the high adventure of this whirling year he had just finished as Captain of the Rangers. In many ways it would be the banner one of all the vivid years that had gone before or were to come. But the search must go on—the eternal search for life and adventure and fortune.

He packed his bags and quietly slipped out of Bisbee. Twenty-four hours later he was closeted in a hotel room at Holbrook in northern Arizona with his trusted friend Frank Wattron.

The next day he boarded a Pullman on the Santa Fé for the East. One way to avoid trouble was not to be there when it happened. If the Mexican Consul-General wanted him arrested for kidnaping he'd first have to find him.

And the wheel of life was still spinning merrily.

·:⟩[*Part Five*]⟨·:·

Cowman

CAP MOSSMAN found Colonel Bill Greene, the tinsel-crowned copper king, going big when he arrived in New York in early September, 1902. Cap put up at the neighboring Holland House and late that first afternoon reported in at Greene's luxurious suite at the old Waldorf.

The Ranger captain was duly impressed with the private kitchen and dining-room and the white-capped chef. The fabulous Greene did nothing half-way. And that held true when he linked his arm in the crook of Cap's elbow and led him into the famous circular bar downstairs.

The Waldorf bar at this time served as a sort of club to many of the city's big-time stock operators, horsemen, promoters, politicians and sportsmen. Colonel Greene knew most of them, and he took considerable pride in introducing his young champion from Arizona to his friends. Cap tried to explain to him that in a way he was on the dodge until after Chacon was well and duly hanged by the neck, but Greene would have none of it.

It was all very flattering to Mossman, yet after the wild excitement of his Ranger days it seemed a bit tame. He had no trouble carrying out his role but in the solemn moments of the morning

when he shaved and dressed after a large night, he could not
help but wonder if high boots and a saddle didn't fit him a trifle
better than patent leather dress shoes and a box seat in a Broad-
way theater.

Greene insisted Cap should at once locate a great ranch that
they could operate as partners. Greene had an immense spread
on both sides of the border and thirty or forty thousand head of
cattle, but he wanted to be the biggest cattle operator in America,
just as he was, for the moment, the biggest copper mining
operator. Right now the Southwest was suffering from a dry-up
as terrible as the one ten years before, but the Colonel still
wanted to expand.

Oddly enough Cap was too good a judge of humanity to be
completely taken in by the expansive Colonel. During the nine
years he had been in Arizona Mossman had watched Greene's
jumping-jack career, first up and then down, and then up again.
He never quite trusted him, but this did not keep the younger
man from being interested in the prospect of using Greene's
money and cattle to establish a great ranch property.

It was the custom of the biggest cattlemen of the West, enroute to or from the yearly conferences with their boards of
directors in New York or the British Isles, to frequent the
Waldorf bar, and Cap enjoyed running into them now. Murdo
Mackenzie, who ran the vast interests of the Scotch-owned Matadors, told him over a drink that he'd heard that Henry Boice,
neighbor of Teddy Roosevelt in his Dakota cattle days, wanted to
dispose of his big holdings in the Cherokee Strip in western
Oklahoma.

Cap carried the gossip to Colonel Greene, who immediately
dreamed out a daring plan for the two of them to build in the
old Indian country an empire of grass and cattle that would
astonish the world. Cap explained that he must lay low until
after Chacon was fully disposed of, and that Oklahoma was a bit

too close to Arizona for his comfort. The Colonel was restless and demanding. The prolonged drouth was killing his cattle by the hundreds, yet he was anxious for Cap to be off. Cap insisted he could not leave at this moment, but he agreed to start his investigation of the property as soon as it was safe to do so.

In the meantime the Ranger captain was enjoying rather unprofitably the biggest poker games he had ever sat in. One of the off-and-on players was a picturesque old Western hardrock miner named Charles Sweeney, who had discovered the rich Cœur d'Alene mines of Idaho, and subsequently had moved to New York and bucked the tiger. He was an habitué of the Waldorf circular bar, and he had taken quite a shine to the bright and amusing Arizonian. Charles, Jr., his eldest son, was at that time a cadet at West Point, and in years to come he was more than to equal his distinguished father's adventurous life.

Cap was well behind in the big game when one evening a bell-hop came to the poker room upstairs and handed a telegram to Sweeney. The promotor asked to be excused. Twenty minutes later a yellow envelope was brought to Mossman. He, in turn, pushed back his chair and cashed in his chips.

"Well, business seems to be picking up," a puffy ex-senator allowed. He was one of the men Cap had under suspicion, but Burt made no comment as he left the room.

Sweeney met him down at the bar, and showed him his telegram. It was from a young man employed in a nearby brokerage house where Sweeney traded, and it warned the old miner that the game was crooked. Sweeney had waited twenty minutes before he had sent the telegram to Cap to meet him downstairs.

The two Westerners talked over possibilities of revenge, including violence, but they decided that it would hardly pay. Sweeney felt a certain responsibility for introducing Cap to the game, but the younger man brushed it aside.

An evening or two later, after a rather suspicious hand had been dealt Cap, he had the pleasure of telling a prominent man-about-town that one or the other of them would have to leave the game. The gentleman looked into Cap's hard gray-blue eyes and quietly withdrew. Cap's luck suddenly seemed to change for the better but he was still way behind.

Late in November a letter came to Cap from Arizona with the information that Chacon had finally stretched hemp in the Solomonville jail, and that it would be safe for him to return any time he wished. Cap grinned when he read the note; he recalled a half-hundred threats that had openly been made against his life as soon as the bandits and rustlers involved had served their various prison sentences in Yuma, and were free to seek their revenge. The cattle thieves he had sent there in his Hash Knife days would be coming out now, and to a man they had sworn they would get him.

His reaction to the very real threats was a curious bit of reasoning: if he returned to his old stamping-ground now, while hate and bitterness against him was still strong and alive, he'd have to kill a lot of people who'd be trying to kill him. If it occurred to him at all that he might be the one killed, it had no influence on his decision to keep out of the Territory for the present. He'd killed enough men already to last him the rest of his lifetime.

But he was ready to go down to Oklahoma as soon as details could be worked out and the inspection trip arranged with Henry Boice and his range manager. Finally, January 3rd was the date set for his departure.

That noon he met Charles Sweeney in the Waldorf bar, and told him that he was leaving on an afternoon train.

"Say, how much did you drop in that poker game upstairs?" the old miner questioned.

"Thirty-six hundred even," Cap answered. "But I'm not kicking, Mr. Sweeney."

"Too much for a young man," the kindly, gruff operator announced, shaking his head. "Tell you what I'll do. Give me a check for $3600 and I'll try to win it back for you in the market. I seem to be doing pretty good right now."

Cap thanked him and wrote out a check on his Pueblo bank. Some months later he received a letter bearing a New York postmark that had been forwarded to him from the bank.

A check for $7200 dropped out of the envelope.

-- 2 --

Cap left the train at Guymon, Beaver County, Oklahoma, and hiring a team drove the fifty-five miles to the Henry Boice headquarters at Point o'Rocks on the Cimarron. The range manager, A. J. Streator, uncle of the famous Albert Mitchell of the Bell Ranch of New Mexico, showed Cap over the property.

Mossman missed nothing, not even the innocent-looking prairie dog villages. He saw that the little mounds of earth dug up by the puppies showed the tell-tale white of alkali.

At the county seat he drove through the makings of a ghost town. And that night in his hotel room there drifted in to him through the thin wall partition the promises of a land locator, "Things are filling up fast, but I'm going to reserve a half-section of our finest land for you and each of your three sons. Get in on this now."

That meant settlers would be crowding in, just as they were seeping into all the choicest ranch areas of the high plains. This Cherokee Strip was swiftly growing out of its initial cattle phase. He must search on, even though the knoll of doom was sounding over millions of acres of grazing land, from the Mexican border to north of the Alberta line.

Someday he'd find the range he sought, where he could turn back the clock a quarter-century and stand off the rushing tide of settlers and nesters. At heart he was still an old-fashioned cowman. Let the others go in for raising blooded stock and bulls with pedigrees as long as a multi-millionaire's will. For him nothing quite equaled the pure joy of pulling up a horse on a hilltop and watching cattle graze as far as the eye could reach.

He hated to have to write to Henry Boice that his ranch did not quite suit him. Greene, too, was impatient at his report and urged him to hurry on with his search, despite the fact that his cattle were still dying in the great dry-up.

Cap drifted down to El Paso and then took the Santa Fé for the little flag-stop where his father and mother lived. It had been almost seventeen years since that morning when he'd ridden Two Bits north and then over the St. Augustine Pass to the Hat ranch. He was a little shocked to see how old and tired his mother seemed. She had borne nine children on various frontiers, and they had taken their heavy toll. The Major was still dreaming of the fortune that someday surely must roll down his irrigation ditches from the Rio Grande for him. Burt did what he could to see that the family was comfortable and secure, and then he went his way.

It wouldn't be so long now until Alvord would be on trial in Tombstone for his part in the old Willcox train robbery. That afternoon a year ago when Cap had made his bargain with the fugitive Alvord in his mountain hide-out back of Minas Prietas, in Sonora, he had given his word that he and Judge Barnes would do their level best to help him if he would come in and face trial, after he had put Cap in touch with Chacon. Cap would carry out his promise.

For the moment he settled down quietly in Phoenix and caught up with the gossip. On September 11th of the previous year, exactly nine days after Cap had brought Chacon out alive,

Alvord had crossed the border at Naco and surrendered to Sheriff Dell Lewis. Eventually Billy Stiles, who had been with Cap at the capture of the Mexican bandit, was also taken in custody. Mossman had turned over the $2500 reward granted him by Graham County to Stiles with the understanding that he would split it with Alvord. But Stiles had drunk and gambled it all away. Cap, incidentally, had never personally kept a penny of any rewards received but had always turned the money over to the men who had helped him.

Cap kept his word with Alvord and appeared as a witness for the defense, headed by Judge Barnes, who was acting without fee. The ex-Ranger captain made an impressive witness.

"Did Burt Alvord help you of his own free will and accord to contact the bandit Chacon?" Barnes asked Cap on the witness stand.

"Yes, sir," he answered. "And without the help and advice of Alvord I would never have been able to contact Chacon."

It weighed heavily in Alvord's favor, although the jury could not agree on a verdict, and a new trial was ordered. But the Tombstone jail could not hold both Alvord and Stiles and they broke out and hit it for Mexico.

Later, in a fight with a sheriff's posse near the border, Alvord was shot in the leg and in terror of his life called out that he would surrender. Billy Stiles got a bullet in his arm but he made good his escape. (Billy worked his way to the west coast and finally to China. Returning under an alias to Nevada he became a deputy-sheriff and killed a man whom he was arresting. Later he rode up to the house where he had made the killing and the twelve-year-old son of the dead man shot him off his horse with a double-barreled shotgun. The Territory of Arizona sent Billy's wife to Nevada to make sure her husband was good and dead. She reported it was true.)

On Alvord's second trial he drew a compromise sentence of

seven years. Upon his release he disappeared, and the tale lives on to this day that he was able to dig up his golden loot and carry it in a pair of saddlebags to the south. Some years later news drifted north that he had died from natural causes in Panama.

Thus he furnished the exception that it takes to prove the rule that those who take up the smoking six-shooter shall die by the blazing Colt.

-- 3 --

Back in Phoenix Cap packed a pistol and sat facing open doors with his back to the wall. The outlaws he had sent to Yuma were coming out a little too fast for him not to be concerned.

He was growing restless and a bit disgusted. It was the first long spell since he was fifteen that he had been without a job. He craved action and excitement, and time hung a bit heavily on his hands.

So it was that when the offer came to him through a friend to report on a mine in the Granite Mountains over near Salton in the Mojave Desert in southeastern California, he jumped at the chance. He was picked for the job not because he was an expert miner but because he was intelligent and honest.

His single mining venture had occurred way back in the early '90's shortly before he left the Monticello ranch. He had bought a half-interest in a silver claim in eastern Arizona from an old prospector. Immediately they started working the claim with several men, hauling the silver ore forty miles to the railroad. They were making better than $200 a week clear profit and they had big plans for improving the property, when the bad news broke. President Cleveland ordered silver demonetized and the jig was up. As far as Burt was concerned, he simply pulled out and turned his share of the claim over to the coyotes and rattlesnakes.

All this had happened ten years ago, and now Cap was once again prowling around a mine. The men who were trying to sell their Granite Mountain diggings were elaborately solicitous of Cap's health. The thermometer stood at 127 degrees at noon, and they urged him not to work too hard in his investigations. They led him to several spots and helped him take out his samples. They even assisted him in looking over the 2,000 tons of dump they claimed was very rich.

When night came the heat was still so unbearable inside the cabin that Cap strolled into the open. He kept going until he hit the shaft, where he lit his miner's lamp and quietly took his own samplings.

When Cap was ready to go, one of the men steered the conversation around to his proposition: they would very much like to cut Cap in on a full quarter-share of the property. They were asking $120,000 for the mine, and that would make his take exactly $30,000. All Cap would have to do was to make a favorable report.

Back in Phoenix Cap wrote the prospective buyer in Kentucky that he was satisfied the mine had been well "salted," and that he considered it worthless.

He smiled a little over the check for $500 that was his fee. It was just one-sixtieth of the proffered $30,000.

For the next four or five months Cap followed his fancy while he waited for Lady Luck to smile once more on him. He joined two of his Phoenix friends, Dr. Bob Craig and T. F. Sparks, and a flamboyant figure from Yuma called "Arizona Charlie," in a fantastic effort to penetrate the forbidden Mexican island of

Tiburon, high up in the Gulf of California. They were after gold, but all they got was a strict order to keep off the island.

Later Cap and two or three companions drifted down to the little port city of Topolobampo on the Gulf. He was vaguely searching for cattle country but what he was really after was fun and adventure. He found both when he and his friends purchased at bargain rates a trim little schooner, owned by several rich young men from San Francisco, who were for the moment stranded in town because they could get no clearance papers for their boat. To make good the refusal by the port officials, a rusty Mexican gunboat was anchored a hundred yards off starboard and each midnight checked the schooner with her searchlight.

It seemed to rankle the proud Gringo, and memories of the long days and nights in the Mazatlan jail touched the tender spot of Cap's honor. He would show these petty, grafting officials what a Captain of Arizona Rangers could do in a pinch.

The California boys left on the first steamer bound for the Los Angeles port of San Pedro. Along with their officially becalmed little schooner, Cap and his friends inherited a Portuguese skipper, who showed the sort of fight Cap always admired. He promptly pointed out to the landlubbers that the Mexican gunboat had no steam up, and that when a black night came, with the tide running out and an offshore breeze blowing, they might slip by and take to the open sea. It exactly coincided with Cap's own line of thinking.

Only the searchlight seemed to worry the Portuguese skipper. Cap assured him he'd personally take care of that little matter.

They did not have to wait long until the black night came, with the tide and the wind exactly right. They could barely make out the outline of the tiny gunboat off their starboard, when the skipper ran up his sails. When he gave the word Cap swung his axe at the anchor hawser. They had a spare anchor if and when they needed it.

The trim little ship suddenly came alive. Cap took his post on the starboard side. On beyond, the entrance narrowed and to reach the sea they would have to pass not more than fifty feet off the gunboat's port side. Suddenly a shout sounded from the boat as a sleepy sentinel awoke. A minute later the tardy searchlight cut through the black night.

Cap reached down and picked up the shotgun that he had brought down in the hope of some duck hunting. He had both barrels loaded with buckshot, and the joy of combat was in his heart. The piercing white bolt of light was moving straight toward the prow of the schooner when he let go. The roar of the shots blasted the silence of the night, and the white light was no more.

They were half-way through the neck of the harbor when the sightless gunboat opened with her one-inch cannon and her mounted Gatling guns. They spit and barked as they combed the black horizon, but they might as well have been firing at the hidden stars.

By daybreak the lusty breeze had carried the tiny schooner well down the coast, and before them lay the blue waters of the Pacific. Cap broke out the Stars-and-Stripes, and made coffee for all hands.

No wireless or radio need worry them in this year of 1903. They would keep well off the three-mile shoreline of Lower California and shortly the day would come when San Pedro and home would give them welcome and safety.

Burt was ready now to go back to work. At least for the long present he had had his fill of cities and the sea, and gold mines and wild adventure and Old Mexico.

It was high time he returned to cattle. He hankered for the feel of a horse between his legs and the creak of saddle leather, and the pungent smell that rose from a herd, and the sound of bawling calves, marked with the deep tones of some old bull resenting youth and joy unrestrained.

Kansas City was the hub of the wheel of his cattle world, and he took off for there. He would look for a job as a ranch manager. He'd get a new start.

The second night after he arrived he had dinner at the Kansas City Club with his old friend Tom Emman, head of the cattle commission house that had handled the 33,000 head of stock cattle he had shipped to the pastures of western Kansas from the Hash Knife. Tom arranged for them to be joined after dinner by Mr. James Coburn, long associated with one of the leading local banks and for the past fifteen years and more general manager of the Hansford Land & Cattle Company, a Scotch outfit that ran the famous Turkey Track brand.

Mr. Coburn was a soft-spoken, highly religious gentleman who had come out from the East as a young man. In the late '80's he had moved 7,000 head of Turkey Tracks from the North Canadian River in the Texan Panhandle and established headquarters at Lakewood, a few miles south of Artesia, on the Pecos River in New Mexico. The Turkey Track now ran 10,000 head of stock cattle, and its range extended from below Lakewood some forty miles on north, into the John Chisum country. Chisum had been dead for almost two decades, but now and again some old Jinglebob cow would appear as if walking out of a mirage of the past.

Mr. Coburn was having a curious bit of trouble with his foreman, Cape Willingham, ex-sheriff of Old Toscosa. The fact that Cape, in his official capacity, had killed a man or two clung to him like the odor of stale tobacco smoke. Dissatisfied with the way things were going at the Turkey Track, he had written the directors at Dundee that Mr. Coburn was not correctly managing the ranch. The secretary of the company promptly sent the letter to Mr. Coburn without comment. Coburn confronted his foreman with the letter, and while no violent words passed between them, the gentle manager was no fighting man and he feared trouble.

All this may have had a little something to do with the fact that following two or three hours' talk with Cap at the Club Mr. Coburn at once offered him the job of range manager. It was rather small fry to Cap after running the great Hash Knife outfit, with its 50,000 cattle and its rustler problems, but he promptly accepted. He'd be back in the cow business, and he was happy when he went to sleep that night. December first was the day his contract would start.

Mr. Coburn promptly left for the annual meeting of his board of directors in Scotland, and Cap took the train south for Lakewood, New Mexico. He anticipated some difficulty with Cape Willingham, but the ex-sheriff gracefully turned over the outfit and explained how it had been run.

The dry-up was still on, and the Turkey Track cows and weaned calves and coming two-year-olds showed the effect of the prolonged drouth. The range was ample in good years but when dry times came there simply wasn't enough grass. Before he had left for Scotland, Mr. Coburn had told Cap about a trip he had made that fall as a guest of the Chicago, Milwaukee & St. Paul to the end of rail at Evarts on the Missouri River in central South Dakota. The railroad officials, eager for cattle shipments, had piloted him over the sprawling Cheyenne River Reservation, on the west side of the river, but he had not made up his mind about bidding for the lease.

Early in March, when Mr. Coburn returned from his trip to Scotland, he was alarmed at the state of the cattle. Cap had better travel north and go over the lease. Bids for the million-acre tract would be opened in Washington on May 1st. The Indian range would offer the Turkey Track an ideal fattening ground for their young stock, and a double safety valve in dry years. The only trouble was that it was far more country than the outfit cared to tackle alone.

Cap suggested they get in touch with Murdo Mackenzie of the Matadors, who kept his personal headquarters in Trinidad, Colorado. A letter brought the information that the black-bearded, grizzled Scotsman would be glad to go over the reservation with Cap, and take half of the lease if they both found it satisfactory.

It was early spring when the two met at the end of rail at Evarts, crossed the Missouri on the stern-wheel ferry and rode by horse straight west down the center of the million acres. It ran some fifty miles north and south along the Missouri River and thirty miles or so east and west, with the Cheyenne River as its southern border.

The older Mackenzie picked a Sioux half-breed to pilot him, and that first night ate heartily of a fine stew in the Indian's cabin and even shared a bed with him. He woke up scratching, and later that morning realized that the dish he had enjoyed so much was puppy stew.

Cap had a French squawman named Rosseau for his guide. By some queer stroke Mackenzie turned to the northern half of the big, unfenced tract, probably because it was nearer the town of Evarts and the railhead across the river.

Cap rode west with his friendly squawman and then swung to the south toward the Cheyenne River. Early spring was in the air and new grass was rising. Quail and prairie chicken scuttled off at their approach, and meadowlarks called to them. The wind blew in their faces, and it was warm and full of promise.

To Cap there was a sheer magnificence about this endless, rolling prairie. It was still new and unspoiled. Plowmen had not yet uprooted its fine, natural grass and turned it wrong side up. It was as God had created it, and there was every prospect that it would long remain untouched by the steel plows of iron-hearted nesters.

Cap pulled up his horse on a gentle rise and his eyes and heart filled with the lonely beauty that spread out before him. It lacked the splendor and color of the high mountains and deep valleys of his Southwest, but there was an abiding satisfaction about this vast sea of grass.

Grass—that was it. Grass for hungry herds. Grass like he had never seen before. Fattening grass; tallow-making grass. And sunshine and water, and the warm wind blowing in his face.

Suddenly he knew he was home. He had found it—the land and the country he had unconsciously been searching for.

It reminded him of that first day he had gone to work for the Hat as a young, inexperienced cowboy, and how complete was his happiness when at twilight he had looked across the Tulorosa Basin, afire with colors and hopes. And that evening near Monticello when for the first time he had ridden down to the round-up grounds along the creek, with the wagons drawn up where the cook fires were blazing, and overhead the low-hanging southern stars were fairly cracking.

Someday his herds would dot this rolling prairie, wide and and deep as an inland sea. Grass and cattle, sun and rain, men and horses—these were the inseparables of his life.

Slowly he pulled up his reins and touched his spurs to his pony. He knew now his heart's desire.

He wanted this land, this way of life. He wanted it to have and to hold: to keep all the days of his life, until he could no longer sit a horse or count his cattle.

He knew he must forever battle with his ancient enemies—the elements, hard times and thieves. Always he faced the possibility of being ruined and forced to quit.

He knew that not one man in a hundred who stuck with cows throughout his lifetime came out on top. One or another of those bitter old enemies would surely bring about his defeat.

But Cap Mossman had complete faith in himself and his luck. Time alone could answer this riddle of a cowman's future. At long as he rode the ranges this menace of the imponderables galloped by his side.

The squawman led the way to the lower boundary of the reservation. He explained to Burt that in the old days the brakes along the river here were favorite winter ranges for buffalo. There was always a certain amount of grass on the south slopes of cut-banks and deep arroyos that offered some little protection from winter storms and blizzards. Cap saw that it would be easy for a few men in properly placed line-camps to keep water-holes open in the river when the mercury dropped low.

He followed the winding river on east to its junction with the Missouri and then rode to the Sioux Agency headquarters. He had not covered the northern half of the lease but he knew there were twice as many Indian and half-breed families living on their scattered allotments there along the Missouri than here in the Southern section. He wanted no part of the noisy cowboy towns, and he was sure that the draws and brakes of the Cheyenne River would be better winter range than the more exposed ranges to the north. The problem was how to get Mackenzie to agree to take the upper half, while he took the lower section.

When the two men met at the Agency it was decided each would write on a piece of paper his choice. Cap shook his head disparagingly about the lower section, and dropped the remark that he wished he had ridden over the northern part. It settled any doubts in the Scotsman's mind and he promptly wrote out the two words "northern half." Cap, of course, got the part he wanted.

They were sections 3 and 4, of 218,000 and 270,000 acres respectively. They totaled 488,000 acres, only 12,000 short of half a million. Cap put his bid at 3½ cents an acre for Section 3, and 3.6 cents for Section 4. Mackenzie's part was approximately equal in size.

When the bids were accepted by the Bureau of Indian Affairs in Washington he was strongly urged by the officials to take out the leases in his own name, otherwise the papers would have to be signed by officers of the Hansford Land & Cattle Company in Scotland, and there would be delays and difficulties. He wired Mr. Coburn, who telegraphed Cap to go ahead and accept the ranges in his own name.

Murdo Mackenzie agreed to pay half the expenses of building a four-wire fence, running the forty-odd miles west from the Missouri, that would separate their two leases. Besides his half of this fence Cap would have to string twenty-four miles of wire on his western line at his own expense. The Missouri River was his eastern border and the Cheyenne River his southern, and they needed no fencing.

He ordered eight carloads of tamarack posts from northern Wisconsin and the necessary wire and staples and had the whole lot shipped to Evarts. Here the stuff was loaded on a ferry and transported down the Missouri to the point marking the border between the two leases. When he had unloaded the material for the joint fence running west from the river, he had the rest ferried to the junction of the Cheyenne and the Missouri, and unloaded the posts and wire for his private twenty-four-mile fence on his western border. Half the posts were five inches in diameter at the larger end, and the other half four inches. He had them set a rod apart, one small one alternating with a large post, and the four wires strung tightly.

It was fall when he was ready to receive his first shipment of Turkey Track cattle.

-- 4 --

It was pioneer work from the start. Save for the barbed wire that enclosed the outer borders of his great pasture, and the fact that the cattle had been shipped by trains to the east banks of the Missouri instead of trailed in, it was largely a return of the open range days of the '70's and '80's. His steers could drift as they chose over the half-million acres of grass.

Cap had never before operated in a beef-fattening country, and the prospect pleased him. The idea of bringing in young stuff from the warm breeding grounds of the south, and turning them loose in this bright northern world of grass was sound.

It had been the original conception of the master cowmen who had trailed ten million cattle and a million horses up from the vast reservoirs of Texas, Old Mexico and the Southwest, into these once free range lands of the high plains. Later daring men brought in cows and bulls and raised their own calves, but at the start Cap figured on double-wintering his steers and dry stuff, and then shipping them to the Chicago market after three summers on the rich Dakota grass.

The old range problems of rustlers and cattle thieves began plaguing him at once. Most of the 3,000 Sioux were concentrated around the Agency that lay in the pocket made by the junction of the Cheyenne and the Missouri Rivers. But scattered along the banks of the streams were isolated quarter- and half-sections of Indian allotments occupied mostly by half-breeds and squawmen.

Their lowly social status and the monotony of their miserable existence, made it easy for them to become minor outlaws. Some of them were downright tough, and Cap saw immediately that he was faced with a situation similar to the one that confronted him when he took over the Hash Knife. The thieves stuck together, and they harrassed him from the day his first shipment of Turkey Track steers arrived from the Pecos River.

Not only did they steal his beef but their own small herds helped themselves to the grass that he was paying for. It took roughly twenty-five acres to run a critter and that meant that every head of Indian cattle that used his range was costing him personally around a dollar a year.

But unlike the swift action he took against the Hash Knife rustlers, he figured that here in this Indian country he must make haste slowly. He appealed to the Agent to help him force the grass-stealers to remove their cattle, but the Agent was powerless. Then he quietly notified the individual half-breeds and squawmen that they were trespassing on his land; but he might as well have talked to the moon. These glum, hard men, with Indian blood running strong in their own veins or in those of their Sioux wives, would only grunt and then turn back to their log cabins. But Cap had learned to take his time and not go off half-cocked.

He spent that winter of 1904–5 south on the Turkey Track, and he noticed that the deep wells being drilled for irrigation along the Pecos and its feeding streams were lowering the water level. It was a bad sign and he had Mr. Coburn sell the 320 acres of irrigated land the ranch owned. Gradually he tightened things up around the outfit and plugged the leaks. Grass was good and suddenly the need for the northern range was far less imperative than it had been at the end of the long dry-up.

Cap advised buying two-year-old steers in Mexico and shipping them to the rich Dakota grass, but both Mr. Coburn and his Scotch directors were conservative men. They had seen too many outfits start plunging in cattle and land when things were good, only to be smashed and flattened when storms or drouths hit or prices broke.

They were happy to let Cap take over half the financial responsibility for the Sioux lease, which was already in his name. Eventually they would turn it all to him and he would run Turkey Track cattle, and Mr. Coburn's own Rafter 4 steers, on a straight grazing fee basis.

That spring on his way north to the big lease he stopped off in Kansas City to confer with Mr. Coburn. Several times Cap had been to his pleasant home and had met his wife and his younger children. The first Mrs. Coburn had been dead a number of years, and his host has explained that his eldest daughter, Grace, who was in her late twenties and had stood at the top of her class at Smith, was abroad. But on this April day when he was asked to have supper at the home, he found that Miss Coburn had returned.

He knew he had fallen in love by the time his train left two days later. And on the late spring days when he rode his rolling Dakota acres and the wind blew in his face, he found it pleasant to dream of Grace Coburn.

Later that summer when he dropped down to the Turkey Track the Coburns appeared for a vacation, and there were long rides with Grace over the Pecos country and into the hills and canyons of the Seven Rivers. And when the day came that he had to hurry north to the great lease he popped the question.

Back in Dakota he found plenty of trouble. He had replaced his first foreman, the French squawman, Rosseau, by Jesse Knight, who was an excellent man with cattle but could not get along with the hard type of men he had to handle. He reported that the grass-stealers were making no effort to remove their cattle, despite Cap's ultimatum to them that he'd made when he'd gone south.

"There's nothing to do, Jesse, but put 'em off," he declared. "Let's get busy."

Jesse was more than willing but he pointed out that he was afraid all hell would break loose. "Them half-breeds swear they'll kill you if you touch their stuff," he quietly explained. It was no argument; merely a statement of fact.

Cap called in his men and told them the story. They'd round up all the cattle and horses on the lease, cut back their own stock, and hold together the stuff that did not belong to them. His men must strictly carry out his orders and let him do the fighting. He strapped a six-shooter on his hip and put a saddle-gun in the boot under his left leg, and led out the half-dozen riders. If there was shooting to do, he'd have to do it himself.

At noons and evenings they cut back the Mossman steers but kept in close-herd the illegal cattle and horses. Cap was in the saddle most of the next two nights. Late in the afternoon of the third day they had a considerable herd, and he trailed them out while he made a quick count. There were 200-odd horses and 1,200 cattle of all kinds and descriptions—and five old buffalo, that had managed to live far beyond their allotted time in the miniature badlands in the southwest corner of the lease.

The Cheyenne River, yellow and lazy, lay ahead. On below its southern bank stretched open country, with a handful of scattered ranches dotting its vastness.

Off to the sides of the herd Cap watched the little groups of men on horseback, slumping over their saddles and eying the exodus like red-beaked buzzards humped on tree limbs waiting for their prey. They had been hanging on the edges of the round-up since it had started.

Cap knew these sullen breeds and squawmen had the wish

to stop him, yet he was gambling his life that they lacked the will. They were dangerous enough but they were without a leader or the real stuff of courage. Still, a cowardly thief's finger on the trigger of a 30-40 Winchester could be as deadly as that of a brave man's.

He could feel sorry for certain of these unfortunates as individuals, but he could no longer stand for the group-stealing of his cattle and his grass. It was part of his long fight against thieves, and he must see it through, no matter the odds against him.

They were approaching the river when Cap gave the final orders. It would mean a step from which there could be no turning back.

"Put 'em across!" he shouted.

"They'll kill you if you do, Cap," the foreman prophesied.

"Put 'em across!" Mossman repeated.

A shaggy, brown bull buffalo, old enough to remember General Custer, led off. In retrospect, he might have been some mossy horn pointing a Texas herd up the long, dusty Chisholm Trail when the West was young. The cattle and horses, and the five old horned links-with-the-past took to the river and splashed across. Cap's cowboys hazed them well toward the southern horizon and they scattered like blackbirds hitting a cornfield. Then the men turned back. Cap knew this would be the moment of decision.

Copper-colored men, women and children, standing deep in the shadows of log cabins, calked and roofed with gray Dakota gumbo clay, quietly cursed the little cavalcade as it rode by in the gathering darkness. But no man challenged it.

It was a thousand miles from the Arizona-Mexican border to this Indian land, yet Cap Mossman's reputation as a rustler-fighter had made the long journey north unaided.

But these scowling, bitter men here on the fringes of this last frontier were always to cause him trouble. More than once in those days he said in his own crisp and amusing style: "I'd be glad to make a deal with the devil to spend ten years in hell for the privilege of killing ten of these miserable half-breeds and squawmen. I could name immediately the first four or five, but I'd want to do a little thinking about the last half-dozen."

Cap stayed on until late fall and it was early December when he crossed the frozen Missouri on a bobsled and took the train at Evarts for Kansas City. Several things were on his mind.

The first was that he would have to arrange for more cattle. The Turkey Track was not sending him enough steers to use more than a third of his grass. He had written Colonel Greene in New York about sending him steers from his great Sonora ranch, and the Colonel had told him to come on to New York at once and talk things over.

The second thing that disturbed him was a letter he had received from his father in New Mexico. His mother was very poorly, and if Burt wanted to see her again he had better come soon.

The third item had to do with the girl who was waiting for him in Kansas City. They had planned to be married sometime early in the year, but he'd figured out a new idea. And as mile after mile of white-sheeted prairie slipped by, the idea grew until it seemed perfectly logical.

When he arrived in Kansas City he checked his bag at the station, and took a cab directly to the Coburn home. He wasn't long in making his big proposition to Grace.

He had to leave this afternoon for New York, and then he'd have to hurry back and visit his mother. Why not get married this very day and turn the New York trip into a honeymoon?

There was a counting of the hours on fingers, and there were near-tears. She could have four hours to get ready for the wedding and the little family reception, and still catch the train.

She ran to her mother and there were flat refusals and scoldings but Captain Burton C. Mossman, late of the Arizona Rangers, stubbornly stuck to his story. They had exactly four hours, and New York was waiting for them.

They did it in bright and touching style, and all in that single day of December 12, 1905.

-- 5 --

Colonel and Mrs. Greene opened wide their great suite in the Waldorf as an additional half-way stop for the happy couple. There were theater parties and champagne-lobster suppers at Delmonico's and flowers and new clothes, and good news.

Colonel Greene would be glad to ship eight or ten thousand steers to Dakota in June, when they could be crossed over the river, and fatted on Mossman grass. Don't worry, Cap would get the cattle.

Then came a trip down to New Mexico, and the day when Burt, with tears filling his eyes, led his lovely wife to the sunny room where his mother lay, so tired and worn. He was glad always that he had made it in time.

Grace and her fourteen-year-old sister joined him in Dakota that summer, and Cap fixed up a little rented house for them at Evarts. They often crossed on the ferry and he would drive them over the lease in his sturdy new Hayes buggy and matched team.

That fall he was back in Kansas City when the baby boy came. Grace insisted he be called Burton, Jr., but somehow the name Billy got attached to the little fellow. Cap's cup of happiness was overflowing, save only for the fact that Colonel Greene had failed to ship him more than a couple of thousand head, and they were only yearling heifers. But Greene promised to carry out his agreement later on.

In late October a wire arrived from Cal Smith, the new fore-man, that an early storm had swept down and a foot of snow covered the grass. Cap saw that there was a competent girl to help and that the house in Kansas City was safe and cozy, and then he hurried to Dakota.

He wished now that he had followed his summer hunch and cut two or three thousand tons of hay in the rich bottom meadows along the Cheyenne. The few hundred tons he had would help, but if the winter was hard it would quickly be used up.

December was bad, even if the Turkey Track steers and the Greene heifers did get some protection and there were patches of sun-cured grass on the south slopes of the brakes and cut-banks. He realized now how shrewd he had been to take this southern half of the lease, rather than the open country of the north. His losses should be comparatively light.

But the long cold spell was an eye-opener. He saw that every year he must put up thousands of tons of hay, that would act as a checking account in a bank to be drawn on as he chose. And he realized that someday if a winter such as that of '86–'87 struck he'd have to face staggering losses. Maybe he was taking too much of a chance. But a cowman's life was one big gamble after another.

Always those two mortal enemies and their helper were quietly lying in wait to pounce on him, and at the moment when he was least able to protect himself. Range life would be a paradise, he mused, if a cattleman didn't eternally have to face these bitter, uncompromising foes of bad weather and hard times, with thiev-ing an added snake in the grass.

He returned to Kansas City around Christmas, discouraged and uncertain as to his cattle future. Maybe he'd better throw up

the whole Sioux lease, pay up his bills and get out the best way he could. The savings of his years in Arizona, with his profits from the Tovrea & Mossman packing house and butcher business, had netted him $30,000, but he'd invested most of it in the lease. He'd probably have just about enough to settle his bills, and if he lacked a little he'd find the money somewhere and pay the last cent he owed. He was tired of the old fight against his mortal enemies.

But he couldn't drive from his mind the thoughts of that waving sea of grass, and the wild flowers in June, and all the beauty and promise of this northern land. He couldn't give it up. It was his life. And he wanted more and more of the adventure and excitement and the long gamble.

Instead of canceling his lease he'd actually try to increase it. He'd heard that on May 1st bids would be opened on two more plots of 330,000 and 390,000 acres. That would aggregate 720,000 acres.

If he could add that to the 488,000 acres he now had it would give him a grand total of 1,208,000 acres of grass. He'd have to bid five cents an acre for the new tracts, so from the start he'd face a charge of more than $53,000 a year for leases alone.

He talked matters over with Grace. If he was going to make the big plunge he might as well dive in over his head. He'd resign from the Turkey Track on January 1st, and go to New York and try to make a formal contract with Colonel Greene to furnish not less than 20,000 head a year.

Mr. Coburn would send him all the Turkey Tracks he could ship on a straight grazing fee basis of $2.50 a year, and so much a ton for the hay that might be fed them.

Cap could buy a few head on his own hook, and arrange here and there to graze a few thousand more. With 20,000 or 30,000 additional head of Greene cattle he ought to be able to swing it. In good years he'd have grass for better than 50,000 head of stock, and he'd need that many boarders to meet the semiannual lease charges, the wages and general overhead.

All his life he'd played long shots, and most of the time he had won. This time would be the big gamble, when he'd be betting not only his own stake but the future of his wife and baby. Everything, of course, hinged on his getting the new leases on May 1st.

All in all, he was in a mighty serious mood when he took the train for New York.

In his office at 24 Wall Street Colonel Greene pushed back in his swivel-chair and swiftly dictated the contract that would put him and Cap into the cattle-fattening business. He would immediately advance $10,000. Mossman would go to the Southwest and Mexico and contract for not less than 20,000 head of steers as a starter. Cap would receive an annual salary of $3,000 and he would put up his grass against Greene's money. When the fat beef were sold they would take out the cost of the cattle and all legitimate expenses, save the charges on the lease, and split the profits—or the losses.

Mossman hurried south and combed the breeding grounds of New Mexico, Texas, Arizona, Chihuahua and Sonora. He discovered that ranchers were not too impressed by any assurances that might ride with Bill Greene, but that his own name and reputation for honesty and square dealing had traveled far and carried weight. Cap's word was usually the only down payment necessary.

He had signed personal contracts for a total of 20,000 head when a wire came from Egbert Gates, Colonel Greene's right-hand man. Teddy Roosevelt's Little Panic of 1907 was on and Greene was so pinched he could not send Mossman another dollar. He must ask to be relieved of all responsibility, and the contract canceled.

Cap had pledged his word of honor in these contracts for a half-million dollars' worth of cattle, and now he didn't have that many cents to make good on them. He was entirely unprepared for this new method of attack by his old enemy Hard Times. Apparently he was whipped before he had a chance to fight back. But maybe this shot in the back wasn't as fatal as it had seemed at first.

Slowly he canvassed the possibilities for help. He was still friendly with Mr. Bloom of Trinidad and the Thatcher brothers of Pueblo, whom he had rescued from the Bloody Basin trap. They were bankers, but they loved cattle, too.

He wired the secretary of Mr. Mahlon Thatcher, the elder of the brothers, inquiring his whereabouts. A telegram carried the information that he was at Bon Air, Georgia, but that he would shortly arrive in New York City for a three-day visit on his way home.

Cap immediately dispatched a wire to Mr. Thatcher asking if he'd meet him and Mr. Bloom in the Midauld Hotel in Kansas City for an important conference. The next day he received an affirmative answer, setting the time. He had now only to get word to Bloom that the two of them were to meet Mahlon Thatcher in Kansas City at the specified date.

Cap had his maps and figures and prospects all laid out when the three men met. He explained exactly his position in regard to Colonel Greene, and he offered the two bankers the chance to take over the Greene interests and the cattle contracts under the same terms he had made with the promoter.

Mr. Thatcher turned to his brother-in-law and told him to go over the Dakota lease with Burt, and that if he found it satisfactory he was willing to go in on the deal.

Within a week Cap and the kindly, bewhiskered Mr. Bloom were driving over the rolling prairie lands behind the sturdy ranch team, with bedrolls and camp outfit tucked behind the seat. Grass was rising and birds were singing and the wind was blowing in their faces.

Back at Evarts Mr. Bloom sent the telegram that sealed the oral arrangement. They would form the Diamond A Cattle Company to handle the transactions, and there would be mutual trust and friendliness. The financiers and their dollars felt perfectly safe in Burt Mossman's hands.

Cap could go on now and sustain his bids for the new leases. And he could pay for the 20,000 cattle he had contracted for, and even buy more if he wished.

And that summer when he rode the green Dakota ranges he could almost see the thin, half-starved feeders put on the tallow and bloom like the flowers that blanketed the rolling prairies.

He could go on with his dreams and let the tide of his happiness flow as strong and sure as the muddy waters of this wild Missouri.

-- 6 --

By early 1908 Colonel Greene was back in the money, and the old agreement with Cap was dusted off and reopened. There was still plenty of unused grass, and Bloom & Thatcher could find no objection to Cap's bringing in 10,000 or more Greene cattle. After all, the bankers were only buying grass and brains. And there was plenty of both left over, as far as Cap was concerned.

They were wonderful days for the expanding rancher. Late winter and early spring he spent largely in the southern breeding grounds buying cattle for either the Bloom & Thatcher or the Greene accounts, to be delivered when the northern grass was strong and succulent. He had commission men all along the border watching for good buys of Chihuahua and Sonora feeders, and trainload after trainload was shipped to the railheads of the three main lines east of the big river. At this time the Minneapolis & St. Louis unloaded at Lebeau, and the Chicago, Milwaukee and St. Paul ended at Evarts, while the railhead of the Northwestern was at Gettysburg, eighteen miles back from the river, with a ferry crossing to the Agency.

Cap would plant himself at the stockyards in Chicago and study the ebb and flow of cattle and prices. If the conditions were

254

right he would telegraph his foreman on the ranch to ship out four trainloads of beef a week to reach Chicago on Monday through Thursday. If too many cattle were arriving and the market looked shaky he would order shipments halted.

It was big business and Mossman was a shrewd and competent operator.

When time for fall shipping came there would be an old-fashioned round-up and the beef driven to the west banks of the Missouri and held on grass. Then little bunches of eighteen or twenty head would be started over the long pontoon bridge that ran to Lebeau. Between each bunch would be a mounted cowboy, carrying a long pole to hold back the batch that followed. On the eastern bank a lane made of snow fences stretched straight to the shipping pens.

During the early shipments out of the lease when he had only a few cattle, Cap would sometimes cross the beef, a hundred at a time, on the old Lebeau stern-wheel ferry. On one trip the flat-bottom boat stuck on a sand bar in the middle of the river and there was a near panic among the bawling, frightened cattle.

"Open the gate and push 'em out!" Cap roared.

Out into the swift, muddy waters they plunged, and men in two rowboats were able to haze them straight across to the east bank. Cap did not lose a head, and from then on some of the old-timers always referred to him as "the man who shoved the bulls off the bridge."

Cap was always glad that he had chosen the lower end of the original lease, and jockeyed Murdo Mackenzie into taking the upper half. But he did feel a bit sorry for Mackenzie the way things finally turned out.

Winter was much harder on the Matador cattle in the open country to the north than it was on the Mossman stock sheltered in the brakes and deep coulees along the Cheyenne River. And the towns of Lebeau and Evarts, across the river to the north, were magnets of bad luck that pulled in the Matador men from their duties.

The climax was reached when Murdo's powerful young son Dode began to spend his time and money drinking and gambling through the long winter months in the tough little river town of Lebeau. One morning after a night of hell-raising he came into the saloon where a former old Matador cowpuncher named Stevens was tending bar.

Dode, waving a six-shooter and cursing, staggered up to the bar and demanded a drink. Stevens tried to tell him he'd had too many already, and when Dode leveled his gun at him the bartender snatched up a pistol and killed him.

When the excitement had died down a bit, someone picked up Dode's .45 Colt. It was unloaded.

It was along about this time that Cap was approached by Henry Boice, one-time manager of the great XIT outfit, the syndicate that had built the new Texas state capitol in Austin in exchange for three million acres of West Texas land. Mr. Boice lived in Kansas City, and managed the large holdings of the Berry & Boice Cattle Co. of Kansas City.

A British syndicate, with Kuhn, Loeb of New York as its American agent, had acquired seven million acres of grazing land in the State of São Paulo, Brazil, and planned to stock it, build a great packing house and possibly even run a line of its own refrigerator ships to England. They had approached Boice to be the general manager and offered him a long-term contract at $40,000 a year.

Boice could not take the job but he strongly recommended Mossman, and got them to up the salary to an even $50,000. He urged Cap to take the job; it would be the largest and most daring cattle operation in history. It would give Cap's restless energy and his roving imagination the chance they needed. Without income taxes to pay, there would be a fortune in salary alone.

Cap thought it over before he made his decision. He would have to spend most of his time on this far-away ranch in Brazil. The adventure and lure of the vast undertaking touched his vanity and his fancy. Never once did it occur to him that he might fail.

But he'd have to give up this haven of grassland he now controlled, and leave these bright, rolling Dakota prairies for a distant land, with strange laws and customs, where the language was not even Spanish but Portuguese. He would have to say goodby to this last American frontier and to the wild Missouri— and he did not want to leave its muddy waters.

But even these were not the things that made him shake his head in the negative. He would have to be separated for long periods from his little family. And no bribe nor temptation of glory or wealth, or even adventure, could bring him around to do that.

He told his friend that Murdo Mackenzie was the exact man for the great role. Boice did engage the able Scotsman, but luck was against him. By the summer of 1914 when Mackenzie had his ranges partly stocked, and beef almost ready to be shipped out, the First World War broke and the Atlantic was closed to shipping, and the great dream exploded.

Mackenzie came back to his Matadors, and to this day thousands of cattle, carrying the brand that looks not unlike a pair of old longhorns, still run along the North Canadian in the Panhandle. Years ago Murdo Mackenzie slipped over to the other side of the big river, where there is always green grass and sweet running water, and winter storms and dry-ups are no more.

Cap managed to see Colonel Greene now and again as the mining promoter traveled back and forth from New York to his

vast and varied interests in Mexico. The Colonel had his own
private car, well-stocked with champagne and fine foods, and
usually he had some eastern investors along whom he was anxious
to impress. Cap, with his stories and gay humor and bright per-
sonality, was always welcome, and more than once he was invited
to accompany the party on trips deep into Chihauhua or Sonora.
The poker game would usually start before the train, with
Greene's private car attached, pulled out of the station at El Paso
or Nogales.

Cap still likes to tell the story of the afternoon when the
Colonel was bound for Chihauhua City with several friends, including Mrs. Frank King and another lady, who were joining
their husbands in Mexico. The Colonel brought out the cards
and the game was on. The pair of admiring ladies were standing
behind the Colonel's chair, and Cap knew that he would not be
able to resist the temptation to impress them.

The Colonel opened the pot and drew one card. Cap had a
pair of Kings, drew three cards but did not improve his hand.
Greene bet $500.

Cap was sure we was bluffing just to show the ladies what a
stout fellow he was, so when the others dropped out he called
the bet. The Colonel must have had a miserable little pair because
he threw in his hand when Cap showed his Kings.

But for all his bluster the Colonel had what it took, and he
lived the life he loved. When he was in the money nothing was
too good for himself or his friends. When he was down on his
luck he had no complaint; he was sure the Wheel of Fortune
would soon stop again on his number.

His two closest friends and colleagues were B. A. Packard, who
stuck with him through thick and thin, and his secretary, Egbert
Gates, who in the present day would be called "Assistant to the
President."

One day sitting in the sunshine at a lonely shipping siding near the Arizona border, Gates presented Cap with a note from Greene asking him to give Gates as much money from their joint account with the Clay & Robinson Commission Company in Chicago, as he could spare. On the back of the letter Cap wrote out an order on the commission firm for $50,000. He knew that Mrs. Gates was in poor health and that they both needed a long holiday in Europe, far removed from the impetuous Greene. Mrs. Gates, incidentally, was a classmate at Smith of his own Grace.

Some time later the Colonel asked Cap if he'd been able to help out Gates.

"A little," Cap answered.

"How much?"

"Fifty thousand."

Greene almost fell over. But it really didn't phase him. Greene loved the big figures and the long chances. He was loyal and generous, but he was just a little too unsteady for Cap.

A hundred tales drifted up and down the border concerning the endless squabbles that never seemed able to more than dent the undying friendship between the Colonel and B. A. Packard, a truly cautious and conservative man. In the early days when Greene was trying to hold on to his Cananea leases in Mexico, he met Packard in Tombstone and pleaded that if he didn't get $500 immediately he would lose everything.

Pack, hard put though he was, shelled out the money. Late that night someone told him that Greene had just made a dump in a faro game in the Crystal Palace. Packard, angry and disgusted, confronted Greene the next morning.

"Now, Pack," the towering gambler begged, "what in the hell could I do with a measly little five hundred? You know that."

In the end Packard became a wealthy man, and the president of the leading bank in Douglas. He often traveled with the Colonel in his private car, and he and Mossman became great friends but serious poker rivals. For some unaccountable reason

Cap could never win from Pack, and it irked the cowman more than he cared to admit. He quietly nursed his grievance and bided his time.

It came one night at the Sheldon Hotel in El Paso, where several of Greene's cronies started a poker game while they waited for the great man to arrive from New York. Besides Packard and Mossman there were A. B. Fall, one of Greene's lawyers at the time, and Hand, the head of his Mexican railroad interests, and Pat Garrett, the ex-sheriff of Lincoln County, who had killed Billy the Kid and was now Collector of the Port of El Paso.

It was Cap's night to howl. He touched Fall for $700 and Pat Garrett for $400. Fall left the game but backed Garrett, and Cap was glad to see the lanky sheriff win back his losses. This was not the prey he was after. He poured it on Pack. He'd win with better hands, and then he'd run him out of the betting and swoop in the pot with a small pair—and let Pack see what a bluffer he was. In the end he tapped the banker for close to $2,000. It took his cash and a check for $1,400 to settle his losses.

The next morning Mrs. Packard was arriving from Douglas to go south in Greene's private car. "Dixie" Packard was a charming and gay lady, and Cap was extremely fond of her, and he delighted to needle her rather tight-fisted husband for his small economies in such matters as flowers and the little generous impulses that women dote on.

Early the next morning after the big game Cap called up the Keyser flower-shop, where he was well known.

"I want you to send some flowers right away to Mrs. B. A. Packard's room in the Sheldon Hotel," Cap ordered.

"How many do you want, Captain Mossman?" the proprietor asked.

"How many you got?"

"A flower-shop full."

"Send 'em all," Cap roared through the telephone. "Send every damn thing you got in the shop."

Within an hour the room was banked with enough flowers to suit the funeral of a Chicago gangster. And when Mrs. Packard arrived she fairly gasped. She could not remember Pack ever sending her so much as a posy of violets.

"Why, Daddy," she gushed, "I never knew you to buy flowers for me before."

Old Pack was a bit nonplused. But finally he grinned and remarked: "Guess I paid for 'em, all right. It's that g.d. Mossman."

Cap did not mind in the least paying the bill for $1,300. It was all gravy money anyway, and he'd been waiting a long time to dab one on his old rival.

Cap had much to be grateful for as he journeyed up and down the border country that late winter and early spring of 1909, searching for available feeder cattle. Grace would present him with a second baby in May. By that time he'd have arranged for just about all the cattle he could graze on his million and a quarter acres of grass, and he would be with her.

Charlie Hunt, a picturesque and flamboyant ex-sheriff of Socorro County, New Mexico, and at this time a big cattle commission man, had long been after Cap to go south with him into Chihuahua. Charlie, who was a six-foot two-hundred pounder, and a notable drinker and poker player, handled most of the American cattle sales for the fabulous old General Terrazas, a friend and soldier comrade of President Porfirio Díaz from the brave days of the Benito Juarez Revolution. The General was credited with being the biggest single landowner in all Mexico.

The two adventurers journeyed south from El Paso and left the train at a siding sixty miles this side of Chihauhua City. Shortly a rolling trail of dust arose in the desert to the west, and then, riding straight out of the past, appeared an old Concord coach, drawn by six galloping white mules, with four outriders racing alongside.

The coach drew up under a tree, and one of the armed guards leaped from his horse and touched his peaked sombrero as he opened the coach door. A little, gray-haired, smiling man stepped out, and Charlie Hunt hurried forward to greet him.

Charlie was deep in his element. He was master of ceremonies and interpreter and majordomo all rolled into one red-faced, giant extrovert. A personal mozo quickly laid out a folding table, and from the leather boot strapped on the rear of the coach, brought out dishes and glasses and white linen and food and drink.

Cap was charmed with the gracious Spanish hospitality of the bright-eyed old warrior. He patiently let Charlie translate every word spoken in Spanish by the General and his own English replies. He talked of cattle and General Terrazas took out a pocket notebook and found the page he wanted. The previous year he had branded 83,000 calves. Cap did a bit of fast multiplication; it meant that his host owned not less than 300,000 cattle, probably the largest herd in all the wide world.

Then the conversation turned to the possibility of Cap buying a few thousand two-year-old steers. The American asked in English how much the General would want for them.

Charlie put the question into Spanish, and in an aside to the General suggested that he add $2 a head to his price as a commission for the go-between.

The General named his figure.

"You are including my $2 in that amount, are you, General?" Charlie asked in Spanish in as low a tone as his huge voice could articulate.

The old gentleman nodded. Cap, speaking in English, said he would think it over.

The table was cleared away and the dishes packed in the boot.

The General made a pretty speech and Charlie translated it, with no loss in color or extravagance.

Cap bowed low in acknowledgment. Then in perfect Spanish he said: "Thank you very much, my General, for the delightful lunch and your hospitality. I will let you know in a few days about the steers."

Charlie Hunt spluttered and coughed behind his hairy red paw, and practically lifted the little General into his coach. The two Americans raised their hats as the six white mules broke into a gallop and the cavalcade rode back into the past from whence it had come.

Never once did the gallant cattle buyer allude to his slight mistake of demanding two dollars a head commission instead of the ordinary 50 cents. Nor did he ever have any further doubts regarding Cap's ability to speak Spanish.

Incidentally, Cap did not buy the steers that day. Later he handled thousands of head of Terrazas cattle, and there was one single herd of 9,041 three-year-old steers from the General's endless Chihuahua range that was sent up to Mossman's Dakota lease by Nelson A. Morris.

Cap and the fine old Chicago packer had a good many dealings together as the years went by. One summer when there was a bad dry-up in the Texas country around Midland, where Morris had a round hundred thousand acres of land, the Chicagoan shipped a dozen trainloads of black steers up to Morristown, North Dakota, assigned to Mossman.

Cap took his riders and slowly moved the great herd in a single trail-drive the 75 miles south to his big pasture. Ordinarily no man would try to drive more than 2,500 head in one bunch, but these were gentle cattle and Cap let them drift south and at night bed down on their own accord.

The third day he had his men string them out, and he and W. N. Pence, representing the owners, took their posts and let the steers slowly pass by between them. The men held long cords in their hands, and as every hundredth animal went by they would tie a knot and make a sign or give a word to each other.

For hours the endless line of cattle drifted by. The knotted cords were yards long, and the sun was hanging low in the western sky when the last steer in the drags passed on. The two men carefully counted their knots. A single animal had walked by them after the last knot had been tied.

Their tallies were identical: 6,501 head of steers counted in a single day and without a break.

Cap was happy that the second baby was a girl. She was named Mary, after Grace's own mother.

This spring of 1909 certainly marked the high tide of his happiness. On May 1st a wire arrived from Washington that his original leases had been renewed at the end of their five-year period. He would have not less than 50,000 head of feeders on his grass this coming summer, and there was every prospect that he would make a hatful of money. And now he had a baby girl.

Then the blow fell. The family doctor gravely shook his head. Grace might not recover. An old Kansas City friend of his own age, Dr. Rob Schauffler, took Burt aside and broke him the positive news. She died when the baby was nine days old.

The Coburns made plans to move at once the motherless baby and sturdy little Billy to their own home. They ordered the nurse to get ready.

"I'm very grateful for your generosity," Burt said quietly to the two kindly people, the tears swimming in his eyes. "But I am going to hold on to my little family. I am going to make a home for them myself."

The Coburns argued hard and were determined, but Burt would not change his mind. He was accepting his full responsibility.

"My little family" was the phrase he used over and over again from then on. Nothing would ever interfere with its welfare: he would cherish it and abide with it, and sacrifice for it. No one, no matter how close or interested, would ever be permitted to come between him and "my little family."

Two weeks later a telegram came from Dakota that he was urgently needed on the lease. Dr. Rob volunteered to go along with him to help share the lonely days and nights. The nurse seemed to be doing well and things were running smoothly at the home.

For the first time the sight of the rising green grass, and the distant horizons, and the thousands of cattle and the horse remudas, and the singing birds and the clucking prairie chickens, failed to kindle a fire in his heart. Something had gone out of it all, some magic from the air and from the wind that blew unnoticed in his face. There remained only hard work and endless problems, and a great emptiness.

At the end of a month Dr. Rob returned to Kansas City. He was worried at the state of affairs he found at the Mossman home. The nurse who had seemed so competent when they had left for Dakota had grown careless and things were not clean and spick and span. On his own authority Dr. Rob moved into the house, and shortly he told the middle-aged woman that she'd better quit. But she flared up and announced that since Captain Mossman had hired her he was the only one who could fire her.

It took two days to receive a wire from Cap with the authority Dr. Rob wanted. He knew a very fine baby nurse and he went to her, but she had long planned on a vacation trip with her sister that would start in two weeks. She could only fill in for that short time; her tickets were bought and she could not go back on her vacation promises.

But at the end of two weeks the tiny fingers of the baby girl had entwined themselves deep in her heart, nor could she close her ears to little Billy's pathetic calls for his mother. And so it was that instead of remaining fourteen days as she had planned, Miss Ann Graham stayed on as a most important cog-wheel of the family until Mary was fourteen years old and entered boarding-school, and Billy was in college.

Summers and falls the little family would be together in Dakota, and when Mary was three or four a home was established in the warm sunshine of the Pecos country in New Mexico, and the move was made from Kansas City. Thus the Mossmans followed the flights of the wild geese.

Adventure and excitement, danger and uncertainty, seemed eternally to be part and parcel of the range cattle industry. Until later years when steel railroad and vehicle bridges were put in, the wild Missouri was a constant menace to Cap and his operations. Whether he used the pontoon bridges or the old stern-wheel ferries to transport his thousands of incoming feeder cattle across the river to the lease in the early summer, or to ship out his fat beef to the railheads in the late fall, the wide muddy river stretched along the east boundaries of his grassland like an unfriendly and armed border neighbor.

Every spring preceding the June rise, and every fall before the pontoons were taken out in early November, there was constant danger from this unpredictable enemy. Custer's troopers of the Seventh Cavalry marching north along its west bank to take station in 1873 at Ft. Abraham Lincoln—and prepare for their ultimate death—used to sing:

> We're bound away for the wild Mizzouri,
> Hi, ho! the rolling river!

And later they added a refrain that went:

> We cannot leave these muddy waters.

As the years went by and the great brown river rolled on, never losing its strange fascination or its evil temper, Cap grew to love it as if it had been a wayward friend. As the old troopers had sung, he could not leave its muddy waters.

He had a score of tales to tell about its treachery, and vagaries, but his choicest one had to do with the morning of December 10, 1910, when he and his little family were caught on the west bank, and a warm spell had made the ice rubbery and uncertain. He had planned on driving by bobsled to the railhead at Lebeau, but the sun had betrayed him. And now before him lay a barrier and possible death trap, 1,700 feet wide.

He studied the danger, and then he ordered a light spring wagon brought up and had a long rope attached to the pole. Two of his most trusted men walked ahead on the uncertain ice and pulled the light vehicle. Two more men manned a rope behind.

Fifty feet to their rear he marched, carrying in his arms his seventeen-month-old motherless daughter Mary, wrapped in a heavy shawl. To their rear came Miss Graham holding the hand of four-year-old Billy, with a man or two behind them.

Slowly and cautiously they walked across the treacherous river: a brave little procession, ready for danger and sacrifice.

To this day Cap's eyes grow a trifle misty when he comes to the end of the story: "And do you know that all the way across, that little tyke Mary flirted with me, when I'd raise the corner of the shawl to look at her."

Toward the end of 1909, Colonel Greene's copper fortune began to dwindle, and eventually Cap and Egbert Gates bought out his Dakota cattle interest for $50,000 each. Later Cap paid Gates that amount for his share.

Cap's association and friendship with the old freebooter was a college education in itself. Greene was an extraordinary human being, bold, loyal to his friends, and generous to a fault when he was in the big money—and always the true gambler.

In 1911, the fabulous Colonel had little more than his border ranches and some 40,000 head of cattle to show for his millions. He was just turned sixty when his foot slipped on the step as he was getting into his buggy, and his $2,000 matched driving team ran away with him. The buggy smashed into a telegraph pole and a sharp stick penetrated his lung. Pneumonia set in and in three days he was dead. But he didn't mind too much: life had been one continuous buggy ride for him, and behind wild horses.

The following year the Turkey Track on the Pecos River decided to liquidate their affairs and Cap bought the head-quarters and the 800 sections of grazing lease. He stocked his range with Chihuahua and Sonora cattle, and for the next five years he operated on the side the West Coast Cattle Company in Sonora with two Mexican partners. At one time the outfit had $110,000 in gold to its credit in a Juarez bank, but when the company closed out Cap had to pay a debt of $27,000 from his own pocket. But it had been a fine adventure.

In 1914 the western part of Cap's million and a quarter acres of Dakota lease was taken from him by the government and thrown open to settlers, and the following year he moved 15,000 head of cattle to a pasture along the Powder River in Montana, sixty miles below where it entered the Yellowstone.

Later he ran thousands of head on the great Crow Agency, paying a $5 annual fee to Mat Tshirgi, a wonderful old cowman whose grass-fed steers were for years the finest range cattle that came into Chicago.

The First World War brought Cap plenty of work and worry and big profits—and no little heartache. In the winter of 1918, two years after he had moved his home from the Turkey Track in Artesia to Roswell, New Mexico, he was knocked over by an attack of the deadly flu that was sweeping over the world. The

Milwaukee Railroad had by this time built a line on the west side of the unbridged Missouri and established Eagle Butte, a little town of "unpainted buildings and painted women"—as Cap described it—in the middle of his Dakota lease.

Looking after his interests there was a big, square-shouldered foreman named Martin Gordon, who had been with Cap for a number of years. In 1913, shortly after he'd bought the Turkey Track, Cap sent him south to ramrod the Pecos outfit. After three or four years Martin hankered for the grasslands and the rolling prairies of Dakota, and Cap transferred him north.

Cap was still in bed on a late winter day in early 1918 when a telegram came that Martin was dangerously ill with influenza.

Cap wired his friend Dr. Rob Schauffler to have the best nurse he could find meet him at the station in Kansas City, prepared to accompany him to Dakota. He took a long chance journeying north in his condition, but no one could stop him.

The nurse was on hand at the depot in Kansas City, and the two took the train to Gettysburg, South Dakota. A car drove them the eighteen miles to the Missouri, and they found it filled with broken ice. Even the mail had not crossed for three days.

Cap gave an Indian a $20 gold-piece to pilot a boat through the dangerous, floating ice packs. He had already wired the Sioux Agency at Forest City to have a Ford at the river bank to drive them across the frozen country to Eagle Butte.

When they arrived at the house in the litle frontier settlement, Cap waited in the outer room while the nurse hurried into the sickroom. In a few minutes she came out, and Cap knew the long trip had been for naught.

"He'll be dead in half an hour," she whispered wearily.

It was exactly forty minutes later when she brought him the word that never again would the gallant old cowboy ride the ranges for the boss he loved.

Cap broke down and cried, but maybe it was partly because he was so tired and ill himself.

His two ancient enemies had been leaving him alone for quite a spell, when suddenly Bad Weather struck, followed six months later by Low Prices. The winter of 1919–20 proved to be the most devastating since the great die-up of 1886–7.

The following summer, 1920, prices began to slide until they reached the bottom of what seemed to be a bottomless pit. Not

until the Second World War loomed like a black cloud on the
horizon did cattle prices ever fully recover.

Cap had long carried an open account with the Clay & Robinson Commission House of Chicago, and in the bad year of 1921
John Clay, a Scotsman who had come to the western ranges as a
young man, curtly demanded that Mossman reduce his overdraft.
Clay made the great error of shaking his finger in Cap's face and
barking out his demands.

Cap's eyes hardened and his voice was sharp: "Stop shaking

your damned finger in my face or I'll twist it off. I wouldn't let my own father do that to me."

Cap picked up his hat and stalked out of the room. The following morning he walked into the office and without a word laid down a cashier's check for $150,000, the exact amount he owed Clay. Cap never spoke to him again, and no amount of interceding by mutual friends or friendly gestures by Clay could get him to break his vow.

Through thick and thin Cap grimly held on to his three-quarter million acres of Dakota lease, and his half-million acres along the Pecos, but it was a losing fight. By 1925 he was being squeezed to death, and in order to escape financial collapse he formed a new Diamond A Company, whereby he put his own ranch and his great leases and his 16,000 head of Turkey Track cattle, and his 1,500 head of breeding cows in Dakota, into the general pool. Into it also went the Bloom & Thatcher's fine ranches on the Hondo and the Wagon Mound, and their tens of thousands of cattle and sheep. Cap held a substantial share in the vast company, and for twenty years he was its general manager at a salary of $12,000 a year, with an additional $5,000 a year from his own Midwest Investment Company.

Cap would never call himself anything but a cowman but as a matter of fact he gradually became a very large and successful sheepman. He'd swallowed a good deal of cattle pride when he bought a half-interest in a flock of 5,000 woolies in Montana in 1916. A storm late that winter killed off half of them but the war prices had doubled the price of wool and despite the die-up his total loss was less than $300. It at least partially converted him to sheep.

Several times in the early twenties when he was buying steers for Bloom & Thatcher to run on his Dakota lease, he had helped them out by locating flocks for their great Hondo ranch and their Wagon Mound outfit. After 1925 when he was not only general manager but part owner of the vast interests of the Diamond A's, he found himself in sheep up to his neck. The company's New Mexico ranges carried as many as 50,000 and gradually the Old Cowman lost his set prejudices and became a true sheepman.

With intelligent handling, cattle and sheep could be run on the same ranges, if they were not "sheeped out" by overgrazing, and there was sweet running water. "Wolf proof" fences, 5½ feet high with two barbed wires on top, and with an additional eighteen inches of wire laid in the ground, changed the whole complexion of the once despised industry. And when Cap would get a bit disgusted at some meat-headed cowboy around one of his ranches he'd say: "Well, what can you expect? A cowboy is only a sheep-herder with his brains beaten out."

In many ways he was now at the height of his ranching career. The great life of the outdoors was still his. And that same year of 1925 a new happiness came to him when a charming young woman named Ruth Shrader became his wife. He was fifty-eight years old and Ruth was a quarter-century his junior, but it was an ideal match.

Another ten troublesome years slipped by, marked by the Great Depression and the terrible drouths of 1934 and 1936, and the subsequent price collapses. Yet Cap Mossman never gave up either the Dakota grass or the warm breeding lands of the Southwest. But the old mortal enemies were pounding away at him.

Slowly the pain and marching strides of arthritis began to grip the sturdy body of this last Viking of the Ranges, as Dan Casement called him. He fought back with all the pride of his will and strength. But the thousand and one nights he had slept in the open, and the years of hardships, and the long pouring-out of his energy finally took their toll.

As the young men of the new administration in Washington began to intrude in western range customs and the use of the grass of the vast public domains, he and his friends faced ruin. It was now that Cap made his last great stand.

Crippled and in torture, he hurried to the Capital and demanded an interview with Roosevelt's brilliant but irascible Harold Ickes, Secretary of the Interior. An order had gone out that all drift fences must be removed from public lands within sixty days. It would completely destroy the fine balance of hundreds of the great ranches, but no one could find a way to check the eager brain-trusters. Cap alone might save the situation.

As fearlessly as he had faced other dangerous crises in the long past, he walked straight into the line of fire. He explained to the one-time Chicago lawyer and sharp-tongued administrator, how the drift fences not only saved the cattle of the big spreads from drifting a hundred miles or more before winter storms, but likewise saved the stock of the little rancher. And he went on to show how the stories hatched up about the cruelty of the big fellows were largely untrue, and how most of them constantly were helping the little man in the round-ups and through hard times. He insisted that the small ranchers would also be irretrievably hurt if this order to take down all drift fences was carried out.

Secretary Ickes was impressed with the forthrightness and clear statements of the Old Cowman. He had never had it explained to him so simply and honestly.

"How much time do you think you should have to take down the drift fences, Captain Mossman?" he asked at the end of an hour's talk.

"I'd say about the same amount of time that it took us to put them up," the doughty warrior answered.

"That sounds reasonable enough. How much time is that?"

Cap did not smile when he let him have it between the eyes: "About twenty-five years, Mr. Secretary."

Ickes exploded, but he simmered down as the explanation

followed, and finally he thanked Cap Mossman for journeying across the continent to present the viewpoint and facts concerning a hard-pressed industry that the Department's own bright young men had so carefully and ignorantly kept concealed from him—and possibly from themselves.

Cap's intervention helped soften the blow, and eventually there was time allowed to meet the changing requirements of the Taylor Grazing Act. Cap had at least partially won his last great fight.

Quite unconsciously, he had become the leader and spokesman of the range men of the West. His wit, his incisive mind and his fearlessness made his the true voice of cowmen everywhere.

When the alphabetic scramble was at its height, and Washington was overrun with textbook experts, Cap sat down and wrote himself a verse regarding the public domain grazing business, and telegraphed it to Representative Jack Dempsy of New Mexico, who had it read in both houses of Congress. It was one of Cap's few ventures in poetry:

I am a gallant gra-zier:
I got out of college this year;
I know mathematics, my French and dramatics,
But what in the hell is a steer?

And there was the occasion of a great meeting of protest held by stockmen, when at the end of two days' argument it seemed best to give up the fight against the powers in Washington and accept their ideas on the use of the public domain. A resolution to that effect was ready to be adopted, when the Old Cowman was called on for his opinion.

His arthritis was causing him considerable pain but he arose unassisted and walked to the platform. In three minutes his humor and irony and clear, bitter thinking swung the convention completely around, and the resolution of submission was not even presented. It was a great day for Cap Mossman.

Honors and sorrows seemed to alternate for him as the years marched by. In 1941 his portrait was painted to hang alongside the other livestock immortals in the Cattleman's Hall of Fame of the Saddle and Sirloin Club in Chicago. Two years later his only son, Major Billy Mossman, was killed in an airplane in the European war.

Shortly after this tragedy Cap was unanimously elected an Honorary Life Member of the American National Livestock Association, a rare and beautiful honor that he shared with eight other grand old men of the industry—Dan Casement, Russell Thorp, Charles Myers, Fred Bixby, W. A. Braiden, W. H. Donald, Jack M. Mason and J. M. Cartwright. Forty-five years before this he had attended the intial meeting as a delegate when this élite organization was founded in Salt Lake City.

By 1944 the last of the varied holdings of the great Diamond A were disposed of and Burt Mossman could permanently retire with a comfortable fortune. He had stuck with range cattle for sixty years—since that day in 1884 when he first went to work for the little Hat ranch as a kid cowboy, and made his first dream come true.

He'd seen it all and done it all. He had twisted the monkey's tail and seen the elephant, as they used to say.

He had handled more than a million head of cattle. And throughout all his life he had battled uncompromisingly the eternal enemies of all cowmen—the Elements and Hard Times. He had hardly figured on these new enemies of Old Age and Illness.

Pain never quite leaves the old warrior, but he and his gracious wife still hold open house every afternoon on the porch of their home, set among the poplars and elms in Roswell, New Mexico.

Old friends drop in, and the three grandchildren spend their summers and holidays there.

Shortly after Cap celebrated his eighty-fourth birthday in proper style, he suffered seriously from a severe cold, and there was deep concern for him. Among those who called at the house was an old colored man who left his ancient horse and rattly wagon in the alley while he walked to the back door.

Mrs. Mossman answered the knock, and with hat in hand and quivering voice he asked about his friend.

"You know, Miz' Mossman, he done a lot fur us poor culled folks," the old fellow added. "And we prays fur him all the time."

It is something to be tough as a boot and yet have the gentle heart of a child.